THE ART OF SPANISH COOKING

THE ART OF

Spanish Cooking

❧❧❧❧❧❧❧❧❧❧❧❧❧❧❧❧❧❧❧❧❧❧❧❧❧❧❧❧❧❧❧❧

Betty Wason

DRAWINGS BY A. B. DEMSLY

Cornerstone Library New York

THE ART OF SPANISH COOKING

1   Introduction to Spain   1

2   Aperitivos . . . (DRINKS AND APPETIZERS)   21

3   Sopas . . . (SOUPS)   43

4   Huevos . . . (EGGS)   59

5   Pescados y Mariscos . . . (FISH AND SHELLFISH)   74

6   Arroz . . . (RICE)   102

7   Carnes . . . (MEATS)   114

8   Aves . . . (BIRDS)   141

9   Legumbres y Ensaladas . . .
     (VEGETABLES AND SALADS)   158

10   Postres . . . (DESSERTS)   178

     Index   201

Acknowledgments

I thought I knew so much about Spain that I could, if I wished, write a book about Spanish cooking, based simply on the many Spanish cookbooks in my own library. Fortunately, a little nagging worry beset me. I should really visit Spain before writing about the country. So I did. I made a speedy eight-hour flight to Madrid on a TWA jet, and I traveled over as much of the country as I could cover in a month's time, eating, eating, eating wherever I went.

It was a revelation. Much of what I had read about Spain I found confirmed; many of the dishes I tasted were just what I expected them to be. But there was so much more! Spain was a far more provocative country than I had expected, its food was more varied and interesting, and the cuisine differed enormously from province to province. I was disappointed only that I could not stay longer—months longer.

That I learned as much as I did was due to the marvelous help I was given by the Instituto para la Propaganda Exterior de los Productos del Olivar (or Spanish Olive Oil Institute, as we would call it in English); by the Ministerio de Información y Turismo (Spanish Tourist Office); by TWA, whose man in Madrid, Frank Howell, a gourmet of long standing, has spent thirteen years studying the Spanish cuisine by the taste test; by my wonderful hosts in Jerez de la Frontera, who not only took me through their sherry bodegas but invited me into their homes; and, above all, by the Alhambra Travel Agency.

I worked out an utterly impossible itinerary, one which would take me to as many different Spanish cities as possible, without a day off to digest all the exotic, strange foods I wanted to eat. Nicolás Lloret, of the Alhambra Travel Agency, patiently worked out a way for me to fulfill my plans, and not a day was lost. Someone met me at every airport, an English-speaking guide was procured in every city, a list of restaurants was offered for my guidance. I could get to only a few of the restaurants, alas, and I could eat only three meals a day, so there is still much I need to learn about the food of Spain. Nor was there time for me to get into many Spanish kitchens to watch food being prepared—the only way really to learn a country's culinary secrets. Still, one enters many Spanish restaurants through the kitchens (and I always lingered along the way to watch), and I did talk with a number of eloquent cooks who gave me detailed recipes for their specialties. In the Basque country, too, I managed to get myself invited to two gourmet clubs, a precedent-shattering triumph, for women are not ordinarily permitted and by pledging myself in advance to eat every morsel served to me, I learned firsthand how much food a dedicated Basque gourmand can put away in a single meal.

Need I say that at the end of this strenuous month I was a little fatigued? Nevertheless, I must add that not once did I suffer from stomach upset (only from overeating!), and while not all the restaurants fulfilled my expectations, the quality of food served in general was much superior to that of most American restaurants, and in some of the finer hostelries the cuisine was truly superb. Moreover, in Spain, as in the U.S.A., the best cooking is to be found in people's homes, as I was told again and again.

There are two other people whose help was invaluable. One was my good friend Ann Tuttle, an *americana* from my home town of Pleasantville, New York, living in Madrid with her husband and children. She could tell me what it was like to buy and cook food in Spain, she took me herself to supermarkets and the big open markets, and she served as interpreter when we went on trips in the Madrid area, capturing for me much of interest that I would otherwise have missed.

The other helper was my nine-year-old daughter Ellen, who accompanied me on the trip to Spain and offered her candid view of Spanish food. After we had returned home, she begged, "Let's go back to Spain again—the food is so much better there!"

It was not, I must hasten to add in my own defense, a criticism of my own cooking she meant, but she longed for the wonderfully sweet, fresh seafood of Spain, the luscious flavor and juiciness of Spanish oranges, and the fun of being served in Spanish restaurants, where a little girl is treated like a duchess.

CHAPTER 1

Introduction to Spain

"Tell me what you eat and I'll tell you what you are," Brillat-Savarin once wrote. The opposite is also true. The cuisine of a people is a reflection of its history and geography, its climate, economics, and most of all of that elusive thing called temperament.

We have oversimplified notions of what the Spanish people are like, and in general quite mistaken ideas about Spanish cooking. What we think of as the "Spanish type"—sloe-eyed, dusky of skin, with raven-black hair—is seen no more often on Spanish streets than on ours in the United States. Spain is as much a melting pot as our own country, except that the melting of cultures began aeons ago. No other country has been the scene of so many invasions, going back to the ice ages, fifty or sixty thousand years before Christ. In that prehistoric era, some peoples were wandering down from the north, others came up from the south, over a land bridge from Africa. Later,

Iberians, Celts, Phoenicians, Carthaginians, Greeks, Romans, Goths, and Vandals all came, conquered, left their stamp on the land and its people. But the culture that made the deepest impression of all was that of the Moors, and it is this oriental heritage of the Moorish Arabs that makes Spain so different from every other country of Europe, and that gives Spanish cooking its most distinctive characteristics.

Who can remain unmoved by the fiery emotion of a flamenco dance, the passionate tapping of heels, the fierce, solemn faces of the dancers, the rhythmic click of castanets and impulsive whirling of skirts? The wail of flamenco music is much like that of the muezzin calling the faithful to prayer from the minaret; it is astonishingly the same as cabaret music heard in Istanbul, in Damascus. But the use of hands, a sensuous weaving of palms from above the head down to the hips, and the costume worn by the women are more reminiscent of ancient Crete. Perhaps the dance is an inheritance from the Phoenicians, as the bullfight—the national sport in Spain for so many centuries—is believed to be. No one knows when or how it began.

The Phoenicians, the world's first traveling salesmen, discovered the riches of the Iberian Peninsula perhaps as early as 3000 B.C., though some historians put the date sometime between 1500 and 1000 B.C. Nevertheless, there is evidence that the Copper Age began in Spain, when this metal was forged into utensils and implements by one of the prehistoric races then living along the southern coast, and the copper and bronze, gold and silver objects which brightened the Minoan civilization of Crete quite possibly came from here. Not only did the glittering metals of this land attract the Phoenicians (it was they who gave the country the name Spina, or Spagna, meaning "Hidden Land" because of its high mountains), but here was also a rich source of salt—quite as precious in the ancient world as gold. The present city of

Málaga was one of the two great cities built by the Phoenicians in Spain, and the name meant in the Phoenician language "Land of Salt." A tale is told in Málaga that when the Phoenicians first arrived along the coast, seeing a fortress standing atop a sharp hill, they spread out brightly colored cloths over the rocks to determine whether the inhabitants were warlike. The Iberians came down from their fortress, attracted by the vividly colored objects, and the first trading between Iberians and Phoenicians began.

When they sailed on to the west, the Phoenicians found still another Iberian settlement built on the site of the fabulous kingdom known as Tartessus, which in turn, according to legend, traced its roots back to the "lost continent" of Atlantis. On this coast the Phoenicians built another city, which they called Gades—Cádiz today—and this became one of the most important cities of the ancient world. A thousand years before Christ, Gades was a thriving port with a teeming population. The Phoenicians planted olive trees and vineyards in the area. The vineyards produced a wine still famous around the world —the sherry of Spain—and the olive trees in time were to make Spain the world's largest producer of olive oil. The Eastern civilization the Phoenicians brought to the peninsula underlies the oriental enrichment of Moorish art, and in many respects it is hard to know where one leaves off and the other begins.

The Romans conquered Cádiz in 205 B.C.; a hundred years later Itálica, to the north of Cádiz and near the present city of Seville, had become the third largest city in all the Roman Empire. Today one can visit the site of Itálica, where archaeologists are in the process of unearthing the foundations of old Roman villas and rebuilding the arena which once was the scene of bloody fights between gladiators. (The day I was there, I noticed two tiny Spanish peasant women, garbed in black, carrying earthen jugs exactly like those of ancient

Rome, to fill the jugs with water from an old Roman aqueduct.)

Yet while the Romans controlled Spain for more than three hundred years, there is little evidence today of their influence, except in language. In temperament, the Spanish are wholly different from the Italians. The cuisine of Spain bears little resemblance to that of Italy, except that the same basic ingredients, the foods indigenous to the lands of the Mediterranean, appear in both.

Before going to Spain, I was under the impression that only in the south, and primarily in Andalusia, did the Moors remain long enough to leave a deep imprint. True, they remained longest in the south, for nearly eight hundred years altogether, but the Moors were all over Spain, up to the Pyrenees. Segovia, a fascinating town north of Madrid, is a study in miniature of the many layers of civilization which have made this country such a curious paradox. Once Segovia was an important Iberian settlement, some three thousand years ago. Then the Romans took over, building a fabulous aqueduct which still stands, every stone in place, towering for miles over the modern city. Goths and Moors ruled Segovia alternately for many centuries, and during that period enough of the Moors married Gothic girls to create a new race—the last Moorish king in Spain was blond and blue-eyed. The Moors did not impose an enemy occupation on the country, as did the Turks in Greece. Within less than a hundred years after their first sweep up to the Pyrenees, the Moors had broken away from Mecca and had set up individual kingdoms. The rest of Spain also was broken into many small kingdoms. Sometimes a Moorish king would go to the aid of one Christian king against another Christian king; conversely, a Christian ruler might help out a Moorish ruler against another Moor. It was not until Isabella of Castile instigated the crusade to drive out the Moors from all of Spain that things changed.

Isabella was born near Segovia, she was crowned queen in Segovia's cathedral. Yet the alcazar which still stands on a peak in Segovia, a breathlessly beautiful fortress-castle, is a magnificent blend of Moorish and Gothic, Oriental and Germanic. The walls and ceilings are decorated in the exquisite fragility of Moorish art; Gothic tapestries hang beneath the Arabic fretwork. The high-peaked roofs of blue slate that top the turrets of the fortress were added several hundred years later, by a German architect, hired by a Hapsburg king of Spain.

All over Spain one finds Christian churches and cathedrals built on Moorish foundations. The cathedral of Seville even has a minaret as its tower. Near the cathedral is Seville's alcazar, a Moorish palace which Charles V remodeled, adding a second floor in Italian Renaissance style. The Renaissance addition suffers by comparison; few other peoples in history were more gifted artistically than the Moors of Spain. Theirs was an extraordinary civilization.

Granada was the city most beloved by the Moors, and it was the last stronghold lost to the Christians. Isabella told Columbus she would give him money for his voyage of exploration after Granada was conquered. Granada fell in January 1492; Columbus set sail west across the Atlantic the following August. Hearing this tale told in the exquisite courtyards of the Alhambra, one can only feel sad. Columbus discovered a New World, but the Old World lost a precious heritage when Isabella's Christian warriors finally destroyed the Moors. At least the Christians permitted the fragile loveliness of Moorish art to remain—for this we can be thankful.

It was not only in public buildings that Moorish and Christian influences remained alive side by side. One day I visited a villa near Seville belonging to the Ybarra family, a lovely old house furnished with precious heirlooms, hand-carved furniture, hand-loomed carpets, enamel and burnished copper of exquisite design. Hanging from the ceiling were wrought-iron chandeliers with cups for holding oil—instead of candles, for this has remained the chief olive-oil-producing region ever since the Phoenicians planted the first olive trees here. On the first floor was a small private Christian chapel with stained-glass windows. Yet when we climbed upstairs, to the top floor, there was a room preserved much as it must have been when Moors built the house. The stairway was so narrow and the steps so high only one person could climb up at a time; yet the walls were several feet thick. From this top room, there was a door leading out to a small turret from which the countryside could be surveyed. The room was still furnished with tooled-leather hassocks and silken pillows, with rich silken draperies covering the walls and vivid, thick oriental carpets on the floors. Descending again to the courtyard, we saw enormous earthenware jugs in the yard which had been there ever since Roman days, and I was told that at one time a main Roman highway, leading from Irún, in the very north of Spain, south to Gibraltar had passed this way, through the very farm which the Ybarras now own. At another period, during the fourteenth century, the house served as a retreat for the mistress of the Spanish king, Peter the Cruel. It was said there was even a tunnel leading from this villa to the alcazar in Seville, though its entrance had been filled with earth long ago.

The Moorish influence is particularly apparent in Andalusian cookery. The spices of the Orient are used extensively: cinnamon, cumin, saffron, cloves. Fruits often appear in meat or rice dishes or in sauces, as they do in the foods of Persia. It was the Moors who brought rice to Spain, and the Spanish way of cooking rice reveals a distinct oriental heritage. The

Moors also brought almonds and they brought sugar cane (the southern coast of Spain has many sugar-cane plantations), and Spanish pastries are syrupy-sweet as are those of the Near East. Yet the *pasta* which forms such a vital part of Italian cookery rarely appears on Spanish tables, except in the form of tiny noodles used in soups or, surprisingly, in bean dishes or casserole mixtures.

Contrary to popular American opinion, the cuisine of Spain is not "hot" at all. Occasionally a tiny pinch of cayenne may appear in a recipe, but even black pepper is used sparingly. The confusion arises because many people call Mexican food "Spanish," which it isn't, any more than American cuisine is English.

Yet the Latin-American contribution to the cookery of Spain is enormous, for it was from the New World that the tomato came, and sweet peppers (pimientos) and chocolate and vanilla—for until the conquistadores pushed their way into the countries of Mexico and Peru in the sixteenth century, not one of these foods was known in Europe.

The period of Spain's glory, when she became "mistress of the world and queen of the ocean," began with the reign of Isabella and Ferdinand. When the Spanish speak of the "Catholic Monarchs," it is always Isabella that is mentioned first; clearly it was the ambition and drive of this princess of Castile that forged Spain into a world power. Isabella seems always to have made the vital decisions. She was the one who decided Columbus should have his chance; she rallied the rulers of other Spanish kingdoms to a common crusade; she determined that Moors and Jews should all be thrown out of Spain (and their wealth and properties confiscated); and she married off her daughters cleverly as a way of further adding to her country's power. None of the daughters, however, could measure up to Isabella, and her only son, her "angel," died before he was twenty.

It was Isabella's daughter Juana (Joan), "mad Joan" as she is known to history, who became mother to Carlos I of Spain, Charles V of the Holy Roman Empire. Joan was pathologically jealous of her husband, Philip of Austria, both in life and death. She had his corpse carried around in its coffin wherever she went, opening the casket to kiss the cold dead features every night—until her embarrassed family had her locked up in a tower.

Charles, or Carlos, as he is called in Spain, was mad in his way too. He was one of the world's great gluttons, who overate so steadily and stubbornly that he died finally of gout in his fifties, having been decrepit and bloated with overindulgence for years before he finally succumbed. It is said he was awakened at five each morning to breakfast on "fowl seethed in milk, sugar and spices," then went back to sleep again. At noon he dined on a lunch of twenty or more meat dishes, followed by large quantities of pastries and other sweetmeats. Two more meals, at sundown and again at midnight, helped to allay his hunger—and to hasten the hardening of his arteries.

A number of cook books were published in Spain during this period, the early part of the sixteenth century, and no doubt there must have been a keen interest in culinary matters at the Spanish court, if their monarch had such an abiding interest in gastronomy. Thanks to his grandmother's cleverness, Charles V ruled over much of the world's land area, having inherited not only the Netherlands and Austria and all the Burgundian lands as well as Spain, but in addition his conquistadores were planting the Spanish flag in South and North America.

When Philip II, Felipe Segundo, as he is called in Spain, succeeded Charles to the throne, he became master of an even greater empire, for he acquired claim to Portugal as the result of his first marriage, and Spanish colonizers in the New

World now possessed all of what is now California, Florida, and Texas as well as Mexico, the entire continent of South America, and all the Portuguese possessions in Africa and Asia. He tried to take over England, too, but his Spanish Armada was dashed to the rocks by violent storms. This defeat was the beginning of the end. Spain was never the same again.

Philip was austere and fastidious, more inclined to spend his leisure hours praying inside a chapel than gorging at table, but he must have had excellent cooks, for many superb Spanish dishes bear his name.

While Isabella and Ferdinand succeeded in uniting the many independent kingdoms of Spain, the various provinces remained stubbornly individualistic, as they are still to this day. Spain is not one but six or eight countries, I was told. The reason is to be found in geography: this is one of the most mountainous countries in Europe, and mountain people have always been independent in every land.

I was able to visit only four regions during the month I remained in Spain: Castile, the province in which Madrid lies; Andalusia, in the south; Catalonia, whose regional capital is Barcelona; and the Basque country in the north, at the foot of the Pyrenees. Each is, indeed, distinctively different from the others, despite the efforts of Franco's government to weld the country into a more homogeneous unit.

Andalusia is the part of Spain which seems most "Spanish"—that is, where one sees the wrought-iron gateways and overhanging balconies of storybook Spain, the enclosed courtyards abloom with flowers, the ever-present Moorish overtones. Andalusia is the home of flamenco dancers, and on fiesta days all the girls appear in the heavily flounced skirts, the mantillas, and high combs which are essential to the Andalusian "national costume." It is to Andalusia that the Spanish guitar belongs, and while bullfights are popular all over Spain, the costume of the matador—the tight-fitting trousers, embroidered bolero, and fitted cap—comes from this southernmost region of Spain.

Catalonia, in the northeast, has remained fiercely independent throughout its history. The Moors were in Catalonia only eighty-eight years, a shorter time than in any other part of Spain, and consequently there is scarcely any Moorish influence to be seen—the buildings are more like those of Southern France, and so is the food, and so is the temperament of the people. Catalonia was united with France at one period in its history; it broke away from union with other Spanish kingdoms again and again. The Catalonians still speak the Catalan tongue in preference to Spanish; the atmosphere is far more cosmopolitan and "European" than that of any other part of the peninsula. Their native dance is the *sardana*, much more formalized than the flamenco, very similar to the folk dances of Greece. Catalonia is also one of the most fertile areas in Spain: traveling through the countryside, one sees brilliantly green fields and lush vineyards, rich black soil and acres of well-tended fruit trees.

Madrid is in the center of New Castile, and by comparison with other cities of Spain it is a "new" city, for it was a small and unimportant village as late as the sixteenth century, when Philip II decided to make it his capital. Today it is flashily modern, with wide streets and stunning apartment houses and so many automobiles that traffic, as in all the great cities of the world today, is frightfully congested. The historic sections of the city are being restored, with good taste and care, to look as much as possible as they did in medieval times, and there are restaurants in the city which date back to the eighteenth and nineteenth centuries, still serving patrons in an atmosphere of antiquity. In fact, one can find restaurants in Madrid serving food typical of every other province of the country, for restaurants are an important part of tourism, as the Spanish Government is well aware.

However, the modern Madrid is not Castile, any more than our own national capital, Washington, is representative of Maryland or Virginia. One must drive into the countryside to capture the feel of the province which gave birth to the most chauvinistic of all Spaniards—the austere, stubborn Castilians. The arid, harsh, rocky Castilian countryside was the birthplace of many of the conquistadores, of Isabella, and of the princes who plotted to turn back the Moors. Santillana del Mar, a town on the Atlantic coast in the north, is preserved as a historic monument to those determined aristocrats of Old Castile: nearly every house in the town bears its escutcheon in stone above the doorway, a symbol of the noble family who built the house in the eleventh, twelfth, or thirteenth century —and, in many cases, whose descendants still claim residence there. The cuisine of the Castilians reflects their temperament: it is simple, hearty, strong of garlic and onion, marked by few sauces and little subtlety.

Santillana del Mar is not far in distance from the Basque country. We drove there from San Sebastián in four and a half hours, over a road that skirted the sea, winding over the precipices of fiercely beautiful mountains. West of Santillana del Mar lie the regions of Asturias and Galicia, where the character of the people, and the cuisine, is still different from that of Castile—or so I was told. My only sample of it was a bowl of *fabada asturiana,* a stew of enormous white beans flavored with pork sausage which I found tasted remarkably like our Yankee bean soup.

The Basques claim residence in Spain longer than that of any other people. They are probably descended from the original Iberians, though when I mentioned to a *Madrileño* that I was going to the Basque country on my gastronomic pilgrimage, he protested that Basque cookery was not Spanish at all. True that the Basques are totally unlike other Spanish nationals: like the Catalonians, they cling to their own language, but the Basque tongue is so different from every other in Europe, or in the world, that Spanish is gradually supplanting it. In appearance the Basques are ruddy-faced, stocky, with powerful chests and biceps. The chauffeur who drove us to Santillana del Mar (and back again) looked Irish enough to have been born in County Cork, except for the black Basque beret pulled jauntily over his sea-blue eyes.

Food is taken so seriously among the Basques that in the city of San Sebastián there are no fewer than twenty-five gourmet societies—all exclusively male. Wives are permitted to attend dinners at the clubs on only one night of the year, on San Sebastián's day. The rest of the time the men do all their own cooking, serving and dishwashing. Each provincial town of any size has its own gourmet club, as well, and restaurants throughout the area offer superb food. Seafood dishes are especially noteworthy, though charcoal-broiled meats are a specialty too. This is the most prosperous and most highly industrialized area of Spain; it rains frequently, about three days out of every seven, so the fields are bright green and the mountains heavily forested—green is the color one thinks of instantly when the Basque country is mentioned, as burned-out red is the color of Castile.

Today, because of tourism and the advance of communications, the national dishes of Spain are available at restaurants in every region. Every Spanish restaurant now has *paella* listed on the menu, though this is properly a dish unique to Valencia; *fabada asturiana* can be ordered in both Barcelona or Madrid, *gazpacho* is available in summer months nearly everywhere—except perhaps the north. Nevertheless, when I asked for *zarzuela* in Málaga one night, I was told this was a form of light opera, not something to be eaten, yet in Barcelona, *zarzuela de mariscos* was listed on every menu.

Among the Spanish people in their homes, the provincial culinary differences are more marked. Economics plays as large a part, as tradition. The cheapest articles of food are always those that are home-grown; *gazpacho* is served in every home in Andalusia because tomatoes are so plentiful and cheap; suckling pig is a specialty of Segovia because pigs can be raised so easily even in an arid, rocky region. *Cocido*, the national stew of *garbanzos* (chick-peas), differs in each region, because in each region the foods that are most plentiful locally are added to it. Even so, in Granada a man told me that poor families could afford *cocido* only on special occasions because it cost so much to cook—the stew must simmer for at least three hours, and this requires an excessive amount of fuel!

There is one thing that is common throughout Spain— wonderful seafood. Even in Madrid, most inland of all Spain's cities, both fish and shellfish are superb, always fresh. This is because an all-night trucking system rushes these fruits of the sea inland from the coastal areas every night. Spanish housewives refuse to buy fish before ten in the morning, because they know any fish on the stands before that hour will be yesterday's fish—it takes three hours for the new catch to be distributed from the wholesale to the retail markets.

An attempt is being made to introduce supermarkets in Spain—*supermercardos*, they are called—but so far they serve as little more than delicatessens, specializing in canned and frozen products which are too costly for any but the rich to buy. The big open markets are much more attractive, anyway. The most beautiful market I visited was the Boquería in Barcelona, where even the fish were lovely to look at, some with fresh flowers stuck in their mouths, others curled enticingly into circles, the smallest artfully arranged in spokes on beds of bright green leaves. They were so fresh there was not even any of the usual fishy odor about them, and each one had the gleaming, plump look of a creature just pulled from a hook.

The same touch of artistry was apparent in the arrangement of fruits and vegetables. At one stand, garlic buds had been strung up so that they looked like flower leis, the rounded top of the bud on the outside, the stem inside.

The odd foods on display in Spanish markets fascinated me. I saw tiny, tiny birds, each big enough for a single bite, dressed ready to cook (and looking, I must add, very unattractive) . . . crabs no bigger than an American silver quarter, crawling alive in a big pan . . . live frogs in a tank . . . sea urchins . . . something which looked like five sawed-off fingers, called a *percebe*, said to be quite delicious as an appetizer . . . an entire calf, still in its skin, hanging on a giant hook before a butcher's counter . . . and dozens and dozens of sausages.

It is because they have so many foods we do not have that Spanish recipes are difficult to translate exactly. I felt this particularly with seafood. One can call for shrimp instead of *langostino* in a recipe, but the results will never be quite the same. The deliciously sweet little clams one enjoys in Spain have no counterpart here at all. Serrano ham, sun-cured on high, snow-covered mountain slopes, is unique. We have no pork product even faintly resembling it.

Because they have mild weather all year round on the southern coast in the Málaga area, sun-ripened tomatoes are available even in midwinter—and what a delight to taste tomatoes with real flavor once more! Oranges, too, are marvelously sweet and put the best of our citrus crop to shame.

Spanish food is fresher than ours, paradoxically for the very reason that they do not have adequate refrigeration facilities to preserve it over a long period. On the other hand, the Spanish cook is limited to seasonal foods, and for an American living in Spain this can make mealtime drearily monotonous.

Spanish meal hours always shock and dismay Americans. Even those Americans who have lived in Spain for years never quite get used to them. Breakfast is early and very light.

Lunch, the main meal of the day, is not until two in the afternoon. Dinner—or supper—is at ten at night, or later.

However, there is much snacking between these hours. An old, old Spanish custom is *las onces*, "elevenses." While waiting in offices for appointments, I have seen the *las onces* tray going down the hallway at eleven in the morning, containing beer, a glass of sherry, rolls, *tapas* (appetizers), sandwiches. One man even told me that our English word "lunch" comes from the Spanish *las onces* (pronounced *las on'-chess*). His explanation: the English acquired the Spanish custom when they came to Jerez de la Frontera to buy Spanish sherry, carrying the custom back to England with them along with a preference for sherry as an *aperitivo*. Since the English have been in the sherry business since the fourteenth century, his story seems logical.

There is also the *tapas* custom: at any hour of the day or night, one can nibble on bite-size appetizers, mostly seafood, at the bars which stud every street. I suspect that many people make their supper of *tapas*, instead of waiting for the ten-o'clock supper hour. In more than one city when strolling down the street with the *paseo* crowds, I noticed bars jammed with both men and women between seven and ten at night, whereas restaurants would have few customers, even after ten. As lunch is the main meal of the day, the normal Spanish family supper is likely to consist of only soup and an omelet.

Dining out at night, on the other hand, is gay, a big occasion, and no one seems in a hurry to get to bed. One evening I was told I would be picked up for dinner at nine-thirty. My host was only a quarter of an hour late, but even at this hour, we did not go to a restaurant, we went instead to a small tavern to have *tapas*. About eleven we went on to a restaurant for dinner: our first course was served at five minutes past midnight. After this midnight dinner, we went to La Zambra, a famous Madrid night spot, to watch superlative gypsy dancers. It was two-thirty when we left, and everyone else in the party had to go to work next day. (I was lucky—I could sleep.)

"How do you do it?" is the question every American asks. The Spanish answers vary. "We don't need so much sleep," one man said (and the number of children I saw on the streets and in restaurants quite late at night made me wonder if perhaps they do learn at a very young age to do with less sleep). "It is so hot in Spain," another man, an Andalusian explained, though it was February when he gave this explanation, and the nights were very chilly.

The true answer is probably that elusive thing, temperament. The Spanish simply prefer to turn night into day.

All Spanish cooking is based on olive oil, and to capture the authentic flavor of Spanish food an understanding of olive oil is important—how to buy it, how to use it. Wherever you travel in Spain you see olive groves, row after row of gnarled, ancient trees, with feathery topknots of silver, growing usually out of brick-red earth. While I was in Spain, I visited the Ybarra plant near Seville, where one of the finest of all olive oils is processed, to learn more about the mysteries of this oil that has been so important to man since ancient times. Olive culture has much in common with viniculture. The variety of the olive, soil, and climatic conditions all have a bearing on the final product: there are over a hundred varieties of olive trees, some bearing fruit best for eating, while other olives will be a better source for oil. Certain areas are noted for especially fine oil: the sweetest of all comes from the region above Barcelona, while in other areas, such as that around Jaén, the oil tends to be of poorer quality, stronger in flavor.

Green olives for eating are harvested in the fall; ripe olives, the only kind used for oil, not until December or January. Workers climb on ladders to "milk" each branch, pulling off the olives one by one to drop them in a cloth suspended from the ground—for if the fruit falls to the ground and is bruised, the oil from it will be more acid. The unbruised, unblemished fruit, gathered in big wicker baskets, is carried to the mill, and it must be processed at once, for delay again will impair oil quality. In ancient times, olives were simply crushed between two large, heavy stones to extract the oil. Then water-powered stone mills were invented to crush the olives. Today machinery does nearly all the work, but the type of machinery used will also effect quality—when the oil is pressed out by centrifugal force (rather than by mills that crush the fruit gently), more air is mixed with the oil, and this causes a higher degree of acidity.

The first oil to seep out, as the olives are crushed, is the virgin oil—the purest, the most prized by connoisseurs, with only a delicate aroma. Then the fruit, separated from the stones, is transferred to another machine for more pressing, through thick filters. There will be a first pressing, a second pressing, sometimes even a third or fourth pressing of what is now a thick paste. With each successive pressing, quality lessens and flavor deteriorates. This refined oil, as it is called, will stand in deep tanks until impurities have settled to the bottom, then it is siphoned off and put through another process of refining and bleaching—and blending. People who have grown up on olive oil often prefer the stronger, heavier oils with a more decided flavor of the fruit. In fact, most of the olive oil in our markets is blended, using blends not only of different pressings from different areas, but even from different countries. Spain produces a good 65 per cent of the world's supply of olive oil; Italy is next, but the Italians import much of their oil from Spain. Most of the olive oil we buy in our American markets has been shipped here in huge barrels, to be blended in American plants. Look at the can or bottle next time you buy olive oil, and you will note it says "pure olive oil," but there is nothing to indicate the country of origin, *unless* it has been packed abroad. Not that the country of origin is necessarily a criterion of quality, because in every olive-oil-producing country there are gradations from very excellent to very poor oil. Even virgin oils differ, since one virgin oil will be sweet, pale, and light in consistency, while another virgin oil, from another region, will be heavy and greener.

Because olive oil is so important to the Spanish economy, the best oil is shipped out of the country. Most of the top grade olive oil in our markets is Spanish. The cooks in Spain, however, must often use poorer grades of oil, and in cheaper restaurants sometimes the oil is so poor that Americans, tasting it, immediately decide they never want to cook with olive oil again. This is unfortunate, for olive oil at its best has a lovely, delicate fragrance and is one of the finest of all kitchen oils. During the present furor over low cholesterol diets it is important to realize that olive oil has almost exactly the same proportion of unsaturated fatty acids (approximately 84 per cent) as corn oil, and, in addition, is a definite aid to digestion and elimination. Animal fats, when cold, cause heartburn and other forms of distress: olive oil, cold or hot, not only is easy to digest, it helps to avoid other digestive ills.

Since the oil is nearly always blended, and there are no indications of quality on the can or jar, how does the poor housewife know what to buy? My own experience has taught me that price is the best criterion, and that the most expensive olive oil is usually, in the end, the most economical. A virgin oil, or even a first pressing of top quality oil properly refined, will remain fresh without refrigeration almost indefinitely—longer than corn, soy bean, or peanut oil. It should *not* be refrigerated—the best way to store it is to keep it on the shelf, at room temperature, for refrigeration changes the texture. Lower temperatures will not prevent rancidity; if an oil turns rancid, it is because of either impurities in the oil or, owing to the manner in which it was processed, a higher degree of acidity (as explained above). Tablespoon by tablespoon, olive oil costs no more than butter, but butter turns strong, even under refrigeration, within days after purchase. I have been using olive oil in my kitchen for a number of years now and would not know what to do without it.

I am also convinced that the ancients were right in ascribing to olive oil miraculous curative powers. In Spain, they even claim that the glowing, clear complexions of the Spanish girls are due to the constant use of olive oil in the diet—and they may be right.

Store olive oil on any convenient shelf, transfer it as you need it to glass cruets with tight-fitting stoppers. For economy, buy it in quart or gallon sizes. Use lower cooking temperatures than for other oils or fats, for it has a low smoking point. I rarely heat the oil before adding food to the pan, simply place oil, onion, seafood, whatever the recipe calls for, in the skillet at the same time. When cooking with butter, add a little olive oil, to prevent the butter from burning and to brown food more evenly. Olive oil does not stick, as do other oils or fats; and a little of it will go a long way in brushing meat, fish, or poultry before grilling.

Besides the use of olive oil, several other ingredients are characteristic of Spanish cookery: a generous use of parsley, fistfuls of it, an occasional delicate flavor of orange in meat or poultry dishes, much pimiento and paprika (the spice ground from pimientos), and garlic, onion, and tomato, used together so frequently one could almost call them the three culinary musketeers. How did the Spanish cook before the tomato was discovered? It's really hard to imagine. The most typical Spanish sauce is the tomato sauce, and it goes into nearly everything in the Spanish kitchen.

Memo to cooks. I have tried conscientiously to capture authentic Spanish flavor in the recipes contained in this book, using what ingredients are readily available in our markets. Whenever possible I have suggested short-cut foods, or "convenience foods," as they are usually called today, because I know quite well that all but the most dedicated American cooks will use short cuts most of the time anyway. Those purists who want to know exactly how the Spanish original was made might take a trip to Spain to get more specific instructions—it's a good excuse for visiting that fascinating land!

About yields. Many friends have commented to me, "You cookbook authors are always too skimpy in your estimate of how many servings a recipe will give. I always double the ingredients to be sure." A smart idea—it's better to have too much than too little, especially when company is coming. Trouble is, if we cookbook authors did not estimate yields at all we would be criticized; when we try to estimate them and our appetites do not measure up to those of other people, we are criticized anyway. Usually, you will notice in the recipes which follow, I suggest the number of servings per dish, rather than the number of people to be fed. But if you want enough for *seconds* (and for company, especially, you should have enough for more than once around) increase amounts accordingly. Naturally you hope that people will ask for second, even third helpings, since that is the usual indication that your meal is a success. And I hope when you follow my instructions for preparing these Spanish dishes that the yields will be considered on the skimpy side—at least, that they will taste so good everything will be eaten, to the last morsel.

CHAPTER 2

Aperitivos

(DRINKS AND APPETIZERS)

With the deepening of twilight, the *paseo* begins in cities, towns, and villages over most of Spain. The population spills out onto the streets to stroll up and down, to enjoy the evening air, to see and be seen, but mostly just to be part of the throng. In warm weather many sit at sidewalk cafés where they dally for hours over tiny cups of bitter coffee or slender glasses of wine. When it is rainy or chill, there are thousands of tiny bars, or *tabernas*, where they can find refreshment indoors.

In Seville one Sunday evening we mingled with the crowd along Paseo Sierpes (*paseo* means "promenade"), young parents carrying toddlers in their arms or pushing baby carriages, teen-agers bold and flirtatious, old people whose sunken eyes still darted brightly. The street was reserved for pedestrians only, and there were many shopwindows to gaze into, but mostly the street was given over to bars and every one was filled to capacity. At some cafés old men sat in big leather chairs, idly staring at the passing throng. Finally we went into a restaurant for dinner. Near midnight, when we came out, they were still strolling, up and down, up and down, though the crowds had thinned considerably.

Any snacks served at bars or cafés are called *tapas*: the word means literally "top" and stems from the ancient custom of laying a piece of bread over the wineglass to prevent flies from getting in. Today's *tapas*, however, are mostly seafood in bite-size portions—especially at the bars. When you sit at tables and a waiter comes to take your order, you may have canapés topped with chicken or tuna salad, or individual casseroles full of shrimp or baby eels in a garlic sauce, sizzling hot, or small sandwiches.

With the *tapas* you may drink Spanish beer, or *vina de casa* (wine of the house), or even, if you are a cosmopolite, Scotch whisky. But nearly everyone drinks sherry, *vino de Jerez*, and for most Spanish the choice is a sherry *muy seco* (very dry). Even Americans while in Spain prefer the pale, dry sherries— then, oddly, they go home again and drink the sweeter sherries once more. Is it the climate of Spain that makes the dry sherries seem just right there? I don't know—I prefer the dry sherries myself even at home. But I have, admittedly, a dry palate.

Sherry is a mysterious and unique wine. Its history goes back to antiquity. The Phoenicians brought the first grapevines to the area where all the world's supply of true sherry is still produced, and they named the city Xera. Later the Romans changed the name to Ceritium, and the Moors called it Scherisch, and finally the Spanish Christians, when the town was a stronghold of Christian forces trying to push back the Moors, called it Jerez de la Frontera. Whether the wine produced in Roman times was the same as the sherry of today no one knows; however, after the vineyards had been destroyed by the phylloxera disease in 1894, new disease-resist-ant vines were brought from the United States to be planted in Jerez, and lo and behold, the wine was the same as ever. And certain it is that in Roman times wine from this same area was highly prized.

By the time the Moors had become masters of Andalusia in the eighth century, the sherry trade was so profitable the production of wine continued without letup, despite the fact that the Moslem religion forbade the drinking of alcoholic beverages. The Moors, who gave us the word "alcohol," apparently found the lovely wine of Scherisch irresistible despite Moslem prohibition: a Moorish poet wrote about it.

> How often the cup has clothed the wings of
> darkness with a mantle of shining light!
> . . . the chalice of golden wine was a yellow
> narcissus asleep in a silver cup.

The British discovered sherry about the twelfth century, and as early as the fourteenth century there were already Englishmen involved in the Spanish sherry trade. Today every one of the Spanish sherry families claims at least one English, Irish, or Scottish ancestor, and such names as Williams, Terry, Gordon, Sandeman, and Osborne appear on bodega walls throughout the area. Even the González family claims a Scottish ancestor named Gordon (unrelated to the Duff Gordons), and the first Domecq, a Frenchman, got his start in the sherry business while employed in a bodega owned by a Patrick Murphy.

During the sixteenth century the sherry supply was cut off as a result of England's war with Spain, a situation so drastic that Sir Francis Drake and his men stormed the port of Cádiz to capture three thousand butts of the precious wine, risking life and limb while the city went up in flames around them. The tale ascribing the English name "sack" for Spanish sherry to Drake's "sack of Cádiz" is probably apocryphal; the word is found in English literature as early as the fifteenth century, and seemed always then to mean a sweet wine. This is curious, because all sherries are naturally dry. Some say the word is from the Spanish *sacar*, meaning "to go out"—sherries for export, in other words, for even today it is only the sherries intended for the export trade that are sweetened.

To wander through the bodegas and see how sherry is made is a fascinating experience, and all visitors to Jerez are welcome. What's more, you may have as many glasses of sherry as you like during your conducted tour—but blame no one, please, if you stagger a little as you leave. A bodega is a huge barn with vaulted roof where tiers and tiers of sherry barrels are stacked for aging. Sherry is a fickle wine with a will of its own, they will tell you. Two barrels of *must* (unfermented wine) from the same vintage, the same bit of land, will develop differently—and no one knows why. Over one a white yeast blanket, a *flor*, develops. Such a wine will always turn into what the sherry people called a *fino* (though, curiously, while all the sherry men use this term, it is unknown in the bars and cafés of Spain, where you specify simply *seco* [dry] or *dulce* [sweet] sherry, or ask for a particular sherry by brand name). The barrel of wine next to it, sans *flor*, becomes an *oloroso*—deeper in color, with slightly more natural sweetness. Taste a simple oloroso, though, one which has not been blended, and it is, to our palates, very dry indeed. A very old, very precious oloroso was offered to me for a taste—and it was sour as vinegar! Yet, and now the mystery deepens still more, when a bit of such an old, sour oloroso is added to another, younger wine, the result is a beautifully mellow product without any bitterness or sourness whatsoever. This is called the *solera* system.

Here is the cleverness of the sherry producers. Each bodega has worked out intricate *referencias*, solera recipes for sherry types. A new wine first is aged two, sometimes three years. At the end of this time it is tested—not by taste, but by nose. A man who has grown up in the business can go through three or four hundred wines in a day, merely holding them to his nose, and so determine whether they are good enough for aging, to be turned finally into a sherry the bodega can offer with pride. For those wines that pass the test, a period of blending and aging and blending again begins. A little of a "mother wine" is added to the new wine, it is placed high on the tier and left alone for another year, then to be blended once more and aged again. Before a specific sherry is ready for the market, it may contain as many as fifteen different wines, and some of the wine in it may be fifty years old. This solera system of blending sherries dates only from the nineteenth century, and the English must take credit for this, too, for they were the chief customers of Spanish sherry then as well as now, and the English demanded a product which could be depended on, year after year.

Now from each bodega there are literally dozens of different sherries, from pale straw-colored manzanillas, with an almost salty flavor (owing, they say, to the sea air where this type sherry is aged), to deep amber, "nutty" amontillados (the sherry made immortal by Edgar Allen Poe), to dry, medium, sweet, and very sweet olorosos.

"Cream sherries" are English by name as well as inspiration. These are olorosos blended with a very sweet, syrupy wine called Pedro Ximenes. They say it was in Bristol that the name originated, back in the sixteenth or seventeenth century. Sherry was called "Bristol milk" because, according to a book of the times, "such wine is the first moisture given infants in this city." Several hundred years later, when an English wine dealer named Harvey wanted to introduce a new dessert sherry to his clients, he gave a sample to a lady customer who exclaimed, "If your other sherry is milk, this must surely be cream!"

I learned a delightful custom in Jerez. For the first sherry of the day, start with a "foundation" of a moderately sweet sherry, then switch to dry. The reason for this is that the very first taste of a *fino* is sharp, especially for those just beginning to learn about sherries, yet after the palate has been prepared with the sweeter type, the *fino* no longer seems sharp at all. For drinking hour after hour, as we do at American cocktail parties, and as the Spanish do during *tapas* time, the drier sherries stand up best; they never become cloyingly sweet.

A Spanish meal, whether it is enjoyed in Madrid or New York or Kalamazoo, should always start with well-chilled Spanish sherry as an *aperitivo*, to prepare the palate properly for Spanish food. Whether it is soil or climate or national temperament, or whatever, the products of a region always seem to belong together. And this lovely, strange wine of Jerez captures in essence the atmosphere of Spain.

(Footnote to the American hostess: Spanish sherry is also a versatile cocktail ingredient. Use the sweet types in place of sweet vermouth in a manhattan, the dry sherries with vodka for a drink similar to a martini. Or combine dry sherry with sweet vermouth for a delightful cocktail, more potent than you may realize. Or serve sherry on the rocks, the easiest and most American way of all. If served plain, the sherry bottle should be refrigerated an hour before serving.)

There are other Spanish beverages that should be mentioned, especially for those who plan someday to visit Spain. There are excellent Spanish table wines, for example, few of which are known outside Spain simply because they do not travel well. The best are the Rioja wines, both red and white, and names to remember while in Spain are Bodegas Bilbaínas, Valdepenas, and Monopole Cune. A delightful wine I enjoyed in San Sebastián is called Chacoli, dry, light, very faintly pinkish, much like a Rhine wine. Unfortunately Chacoli will not travel at all, not even to other parts of Spain, so it is not to be found anywhere but in the Basque country where it is produced.

Spanish champagne can be surprisingly good—at least, that was my experience, though I have been told that some of the Spanish champagnes are much too sweet. There are a number of very sweet still wines, of which the best known are those of Málaga. Lacrima Christi, "Christ's Tear," pleases those who like syrupy wines. And of course, too, there is Spanish brandy, produced by the solera system in Jerez, alongside the sherries in each of the bodegas. The Spanish brandies tend to be sweeter and heavier than French cognacs, but the Spanish people love them, and dozens of different brandies are to be had at every bar and sidewalk café. Have one with coffee (or in your coffee) while sitting in the sun of a late spring day, perfect with one of the many little very sweet confections sold at Spanish pastry shops. Terry's Centenario is one of the most popular, Domecq's Fundador probably the most famous, and González's Lepanto is the most expensive. Just as with sherries, the thing to do with Spanish brandies is to taste several until you find one to your particular taste.

Naturally all these native wines and spirits are much used in Spanish cooking—sherry in particular.

One of the most delightful places to go for *aperitivos* in Madrid is a tavern called Gayango, where one sits on small, upturned wine casks in a cheerful room whose walls are plastered with posters of Goya sketches. The menu at Gayango lists some sixty different tapas. Many are made with products found only in Spain: *chanquetes*—tiny sardines no longer than a thumbnail, crisply fried; *anguillas*—miniature eels looking like gray spaghetti, hot and garlicky, which you must eat with a wooden fork; *morcilla de mi pueblo*—black sausage crunchy with pine nuts (*piñones*); and *calamaritos*—squid served in its own black ink. Fortunately, there still remain many tapas that can be translated into American ingredients—and some of the recipes that follow are adapted from appetizers I enjoyed at Gayango.

With all the variety of tapas to choose from, most people end by selecting olives, salted almonds, and shrimp—and these three are, after all, the best accompaniments to *vino de Jerez,* wherever and whenever tapas time is enjoyed.

Drinks

ANDALUZ

Americans may be more familiar with this drink by the name "Spanish screwdriver." It consists simply of sherry and orange juice, in whatever proportions are convenient. For a tall drink, it may be only a jigger of sherry, a few ice cubes, then orange juice to fill the glass (or orange juice and soda). Or, for a cocktail, the combination may consist of equal quantities of sherry and orange juice, with shaved ice. In Spain, a dry sherry will be used, though any of the sweeter types are equally good. Sherry does miraculous things to orange juice.

SISYPHUS

Americans on the island of Majorca invented this one. Fill an old-fashioned glass with crushed ice. Over the ice pour very dry sherry. Garnish with thin slices of Spanish melon or cantaloupe. A sprig of mint in the top of each is pretty, but not essential.

SANGRIA

There are dozens of recipes for Sangría, the one ingredient common to all of them being dry red wine. Most frequently in Spain, it seems to be simply red wine, soda, and a spiral of

orange peel. I prefer the following version myself. Lovely for
a summer luncheon.

1 bottle (fifth) dry red wine
Juice ½ lemon
Juice 1 orange
1 package frozen peaches,
  with syrup

Spiral of orange peel or cucumber rind
Ice cubes, soda

Combine the wine with fruit juices and peaches. Let stand
until peaches are defrosted. Pour into tall pitcher, add 6 to 8
ice cubes and the orange peel. Fill pitcher with club soda.
Makes about 10 servings; allow 2 or 3 servings per person.

BASQUE LINOYADA

1 bottle dry white wine
1 bottle dry red wine
Rind of 6 lemons

Juice of 1 lemon
1 cup sugar, or to taste
1 cup water

Ice cubes

Add lemon rind and juice to the wine with sugar; let stand
in refrigerator overnight. Fill with cubes and water before serving. Makes 16 servings; allow at least 2 servings per person.

Tapas

GAMBAS AL AJILLO (Shrimp with Garlic)

1½ pounds small raw shrimp,
  in the shell
¾ cup olive oil

2 or 3 garlic cloves
1 tablespoon minced parsley
½ teaspoon salt

Shell shrimp, leaving tails on. Place with remaining ingredients in a bowl, leaving the garlic buds whole, marinate
at least 1 hour, up to 5 or 6 hours, then place in an oven
preheated to 450° F. and cook 5 to 7 minutes, just until
shrimp are pink. Remove garlic buds, serve shrimp in the

casserole in which they cooked, to be speared with tooth-picks while still sizzling hot. In Spain they are served in individual earthenware casseroles. If preferred, the shrimp can be cooked in the oil at table in an electric skillet or over a *hibachi* or other table grill. Avoid overcooking. Small shrimp run 20 to 25 shrimp to the pound; allow 2 to 3 for each person as appetizers.

ALMEJAS A LA MARINERA (Clams à la Marinera)

In Spain these are made with tiny clams in the shell, cooked in a spicy, garlicky sauce. Canned clams may be used for this Americanized version.

1 *quart cherrystone clams in the shell, or*	2 *pimientos, minced*
	1 *small onion, minced*
1 *can (10 ounces) whole clams*	½ *cup canned tomatoes or tomato sauce*
¼ *cup olive oil*	2 *tablespoons medium sherry*
2 *or 3 garlic cloves, minced*	¼ *cup minced parsley*

Sauté garlic, pimiento, and onion in olive oil in skillet until tender; add tomatoes or sauce, sherry, and strained clam juice, cook until reduced and thickened. Add clams, cook 3 to 5 minutes (or until clamshells have opened). Add parsley during last minute. Serve hot from the dish in which they cooked.

ENSALADA DE ATUN (Tuna Salad)

1 *can (7 ounces) tuna fish, drained*	1 *medium onion, thinly sliced*
	2 *tablespoons minced parsley*
1 *tablespoon Spanish olive oil*	*Few drops lemon juice*

Rinse tuna quickly under warm water, add fresh olive oil and remaining ingredients, toss to blend. Serve with bread or crackers, or sauté bread squares in olive oil, top bread with the tuna mixture, garnish each with a slice of pimiento-stuffed olive.

TOASTED ALMONDS

Blanch almonds by covering with boiling water, let stand 5 minutes, peel off skins. If skins do not come off easily, cover with more boiling water. Spread almonds on shallow pan, place in moderate oven until lightly browned, let cool. Toss with a little olive oil and sprinkle with salt. For variation, add a dusting of cumin powder or crushed coriander to the salt. Always a perfect complement to sherry.

GAMBAS AL JEREZ (Shrimp in Sherry Sauce)

1 *pound small already shelled raw shrimp*
¼ *cup olive oil*
2 *or 3 garlic cloves, peeled*
½ *teaspoon salt*
¼ *cup dry sherry*
1 *tablespoon minced parsley*

Combine all ingredients. Marinate several hours. Remove garlic cloves, heat in saucepan or electric skillet or under broiler until shrimp have just turned pink. Serve hot, with toothpicks. Should be 20 to 25 shrimp to the pound, enough to serve 7 to 10 persons.

(*Note:* This dressing is also good served over cold boiled shrimp; marinate the shrimp *after* cooking for several hours.)

LANGOSTINOS VINAGRETA (Shrimp Vinaigrette)

1½ *pounds medium raw shrimp in the shell, or 3 cans large shrimp, drained*
¼ *cup vinegar*
2 *tablespoons olive oil*
½ *teaspoon salt*
Dash of Tabasco sauce or cayenne
2 *egg yolks, hard-cooked, minced*
1 *tablespoon minced parsley*
2 *tablespoons finely minced green pepper*
2 *tablespoons capers*
1 *tablespoon grated onion*

Cook and shell fresh shrimp. Combine all ingredients, marinate at least 6 hours. Serve cold. Serves 6 to 8 persons.

SARDINAS EN CAZUELA (Sardines in Casserole)

2 cans imported sardines
½ cup olive oil
2 large onions, chopped

1 small can (4 ounces)
  pimientos, cut in strips
Salt to taste

Rinse sardines quickly under warm water; drain. Pour half the olive oil over bottom of shallow casserole. Place a layer of chopped onions over the oil, then arrange sardines and pimiento over the onion. Cover with remaining oil. Sprinkle lightly with salt. Bake at 350° F. for 30 minutes. Serve hot from the casserole with forks and crusty bread to scoop up the sauce. Astonishingly good. (I hesitate to give servings for this, for once I ate half the casserole all by myself. It *should* be enough, as an appetizer, for 4 to 6 persons.)

HUEVOS RELLENOS (Stuffed Eggs)

6 hard-cooked eggs
6 anchovy fillets, minced
1 tablespoon minced parsley

3 tablespoons mayonnaise
Salt and pepper to taste
6 strips pimiento

Cut eggs in half, carefully removing yolks. Mash yolks with a fork, add anchovy, parsley, mayonnaise, and seasonings, blending well. Refill whites, piling lightly. Lay a strip of pimiento across the top of each. Chill. Makes 12.

HIGADOS DE POLLO (Chicken Livers Brochette)

Chicken livers are marinated in olive oil and a little grated onion for at least half an hour, then removed from the oil, run on a small skewer, and sprinkled with salt and pepper. Grill over charcoal until well-browned, serve at once.

MEDIANOCHES (Sandwich Snacks)

These were served as tapas when I was in Jerez. The name means "midnights." Thin slices of ham—in Spain it would be their luscious dark red Serrano ham—are served in small, soft buttered rolls. In other words, bite-size ham sandwiches!

LENGUADOS FRITOS (Fried Sole)

Cut 1 pound fillets of sole into pieces ½ inch wide by 1½ inches long. Dip each into the following batter: Beat 2 egg whites until stiff. Separately beat the egg yolks with ¼ cup flour, 2 tablespoons water, and ¼ teaspoon salt. Fold beaten whites into the yolk mixture, stirring gently until smooth. Heat oil in an electric skillet or electric deep-fat fryer, setting controls at 375°. When ready to serve, dip the slivers of fish into the batter, fry in hot fat until crisp on both sides. Serve immediately. Makes about 30 bite-size pieces.

DELICIAS DE QUESO (Cheese Delights)

Blend 6 ounces soft cheese (or grate the same amount of hard cheese) with ¾ cup flour and 4 tablespoons (½ stick) butter softened to room temperature. Form into small balls, rubbing between the palms of your hands, then roll each ball in fine dry crumbs. Place on aluminum foil or oven baking sheet. These can be made up hours in advance and left in refrigerator. When ready to serve, place in preheated 350° oven for 15 minutes, until golden, turning once. Serve hot. Makes about 20.

EMPAREDADOS DE JAMON Y QUESO
(Ham and Cheese Canapés)

Spread a slice of white bread (crusts removed) with mayonnaise. Lay a piece of thin ham over the mayonnaise, then a slice of sharp cheese over the ham. Place under broiler until cheese is melted. Serve hot.

SALMON AHUMADO (Smoked Salmon)

This is simply smoked salmon which has been marinated in olive oil, served with a dressing of capers and minced hard-cooked egg yolk.

LEMON-STUFFED OLIVES

Buy martini olives; drain, stuff into the holes tiny bits of lemon peel. (For variation, use orange peel as stuffing for other olives.) Cover with the following marinade: 1 cup dry white wine, 1 cup water, 1 tablespoon white vinegar, 1 tablespoon olive oil, ¼ teaspoon thyme, crumbled into powder between fingers, pinch of powdered fennel, pinch of basil. Let olives stand in this mixture 24 to 48 hours before serving.

ENSALADILLA RUSSA (Russian Salad Canapé)

Cut white bread into squares (trimming crusts), sauté in olive oil until delicately browned. Spread a spoonful of the following mixture over each bread square: Blend together 2 cups cooked peas, 1 cup tiny cubes of cooked carrots, 1 pimiento, minced, 1 tablespoon grated onion, and ½ cup mayonnaise. Add salt and other seasonings to taste. Garnish each canapé with a strip of pimiento. The salad mixture can be prepared the preceding morning, but do not spread on the sautéed toast squares until an hour before guests are due.

ENSALADILLA DE ALMEJAS (Clam Salad)

1 can (7 ounces) minced clams

1 green pepper, minced fine

2 slices onion, minced

¼ cup chopped green olives

2 tablespoons fresh mayonnaise or ali-oli Sauce (see Index for both)

Drain clams, combine with remaining ingredients. Serve as a topping for sautéed bread squares or as a dip. If mayonnaise is used, first rub mixing bowl with a cut clove of garlic before adding remaining ingredients.

ENSALADILLA DE POLLO (Chicken Salad)

1 *cup diced cooked chicken*
2 *pimientos, minced*

½ *cup cooked peas*
Pinch *of cumin*
Mayonnaise

Combine ingredients, using only enough mayonnaise to hold ingredients together. Serve as a spread or on squares of sautéed bread.

ALBONDIGAS (Meat Balls)

1 *pound lean meat, ground*
1 *or 2 garlic cloves, crushed*
1 *tablespoon minced parsley*

¾ *teaspoon salt*
1 *tablespoon olive oil*
½ *cup fine bread crumbs*
1 *egg, beaten*

Blend together all ingredients, kneading with fingers until smooth. Form into ½-inch balls, sauté in additional olive oil until well browned on all sides. Serve hot on toothpicks. Makes about 25.

EMPANADITAS DE TERNERA (Veal Pastries)

Use 2 packages pie-crust mix, or make pastry by your favorite recipe, using 3 cups flour. Divide in 4 or 6 parts, rolling out to ⅛-inch thickness, just as for piecrust, cutting circles with biscuit cutter. Place a teaspoonful of filling (see below) in each, topping with second round, then crimp edges to seal. Bake at 400° for 25 minutes, or deep-fat fry until crisp and brown (375°). Makes 20 to 25 little pastries.

FILLING

¾ pound boned breast of veal,   2 pimientos, chopped
   or ground meat-loaf mixture   ¾ teaspoon salt
2 medium onions, minced   2 tablespoons white wine
4 tablespoons olive oil

Mince veal with sharp knife, or have butcher put once through food grinder. Sauté onions in olive oil until tender; add pimientos, cook 3 minutes. Add veal, salt, and wine, cook 5 minutes longer.

BUNUELITOS DE JAMON (Ham Fritters)

2 eggs, separated   2 cups cooked ground ham
2 tablespoons flour   Pinch of salt
2 tablespoons milk   Dash of pepper
   Oil for frying

Beat egg whites until stiff. Separately beat together yolks, flour, milk, salt and pepper; add the ground ham, fold in the whites. Drop by spoonfuls into oil, heated to 365°, until golden on all sides. Serve hot. Makes 2 dozen.

DATILES CON BACON (Dates with Bacon)

Roll pitted dates with half slices of bacon. Place under broiler, turning once, until bacon is crisp. Serve hot. Especially good with amontillado sherry.

GAMBAS EMPANADAS (Batter-Fried Shrimp)

For 1 pound already shelled, deveined raw shrimp prepare the following batter. Dip shrimp in batter, fry until puffed and crisp in oil preheated to 360°. Serve with ali-oli, salsa verde (see Index for both), or mustard sauce.

BATTER

2 *cups sifted flour*
3 *teaspoons baking powder*
½ *teaspoon salt*

2 *eggs, beaten*
¾ *cup milk*

Sift together flour, baking powder, and salt, beat in eggs and milk until smooth. Batter should be thick. Dip shrimp in batter until well coated. Serves 6 to 8 persons as an appetizer.

TARTA DE CEBOLLA (Onion Tart)

1 *package hot-roll mix*
2 *pounds yellow onions*
½ *cup olive oil*

1 *teaspoon salt*
2 *pimientos, cut in strips*
10 *to 14 pitted black olives*

Follow directions on side of hot-roll mix package for pizza dough; roll out to fit two 9-inch pie pans. Peel, slice, and chop onions, simmer in olive oil over moderate to low heat for 40 minutes until so soft they are almost a purée—but do not allow to brown. Add salt. Divide onion purée in two parts, fill the two unbaked dough shells with the mixture. Arrange strips of pimiento and the black olives (preferably the wrinkled Italian or Greek olives) in a pattern over the onions. Bake in preheated 450° oven for 15 minutes. Cut in wedges to serve. Good either hot or cold. Superb with a very dry sherry, such as Tío Pepe or La Ina. Also good with beer.

Tapas are the between-meal snacks, the cocktail appetizers, the finger foods of Spain. A selection of hors d'oeuvres served at the beginning of a meal is called *entremeses*. Inevitably there is considerable overlapping. Some of the recipes given above for tapas could as easily be served as entremeses, and the recipes for entremeses that follow could also be offered with sherry at the cocktail hour.

Entremeses

TOMATES RELLENOS (Stuffed Tomatoes)

Use small whole tomatoes, slightly larger than the cherry tomatoes, scooping out enough of the top to fill with a stuffing. Serve as an edging around a platter of cold fish masked with mayonnaise, or a *prensado de carne* (see Index).

Onion Stuffing: Combine 1 tablespoon minced onion, 1 crushed garlic clove, 1 teaspoon minced parsley, and 2 tablespoons mayonnaise. Blend thoroughly. Especially good if mayonnaise is freshly made, with Spanish olive oil.

Ham Stuffing: Combine ¼ cup minced cooked ham, 1 teaspoon grated onion, 1 tablespoon minced green pepper, 2 tablespoons mayonnaise.

Anchovy Stuffing: Mince 2 anchovy fillets, add to ¼ cup mayonnaise with 1 teaspoon grated onion and 1 crushed garlic clove. Garnish with minced parsley.

ENSALADA DE LANGOSTA (Lobster Salad)

1 *cup diced cooked lobster meat*	2 *stalks celery, minced*
4 *chopped pimiento-stuffed olives*	*Freshly made Spanish mayonnaise (see Index)*
2 *teaspoons capers*	3 *hard-cooked eggs*

Combine lobster, olives, capers, and celery, blend with mayonnaise. Arrange on lettuce surrounded by eggs cut in wedges. At a buffet this can be one of several offerings, or alone as a luncheon dish it is just one good serving.

TOMATES ALI-OLI

Arrange quartered tomatoes, hard-boiled eggs, strips of ham, and strips of green pepper on salad plates, garnish with ali-oli sauce (see Index).

PRENSADO DE CARNE (Meat Pâté)

½ cup ground cooked ham
2 pounds ground lean beef
1 small onion, peeled, ground
2 tablespoons fine dry crumbs
⅓ cup medium dry sherry
1½ teaspoons salt

Dash of pepper
1 egg, beaten
½ pound Canadian bacon, thinly sliced
1 cup clarified stock or bouillon
2 bay leaves

Combine ground ham and beef with onion, bread crumbs, and sherry; season with salt and pepper. Add egg, blend well. Place overlapping slices of bacon on cheesecloth; pat meat mixture over bacon. Roll into fat cylinder, cover with cheesecloth, tie at ends. Put on rack in kettle or large skillet, add stock and bay leaves. Simmer, covered, 1½ hours. Remove roll, chill slightly, remove cheesecloth. Cover meat with glaze as directed. Serves 10 to 12 as an appetizer.

GLAZE

¼ cup white wine or sherry
¼ teaspoon mixed herbs
2 teaspoons unflavored gelatin

2 tablespoons cold water
½ cup boiling water
¼ teaspoon salt

Combine wine and herbs, marinate ½ hour; strain. Add gelatin to cold water to soften, dissolve with boiling water, add salt and herb-flavored wine. Chill until consistency of unbeaten egg white, spoon over meat roll. When firm, repeat. To serve, slice glazed meat roll thinly, serve like a *pâté*.

PRENSADO DE PESCADO (Fish Pâté)

1 3-pound sea bass, filleted
1 or 2 garlic cloves, minced
1/4 cup minced onion
1 tablespoon minced parsley
2 tablespoons fine dry crumbs

1 egg, beaten
Salt, pepper to taste
1/4 pound thin-sliced boiled
    ham

Ask your fishman to fillet the bass, saving the bones. With these make stock, adding an onion, half a carrot, and 1/2 teaspoon salt for 2 cups water; boil 1/2 hour, strain, set aside. Put the raw fish through a food grinder, or chop with sharp knife. Combine with garlic, onion, parsley, crumbs, egg, salt and pepper. Form with fingers into smooth mixture. Place cheesecloth on a board, then lay ham in overlapping slices in center. Place fish mixture on ham. Roll up cheesecloth, pressing into firm roll, tying cheesecloth at ends. Place in kettle, cover with the clear stock, cook for 45 minutes. Cool slightly, remove the *prensado*, chill in the cheesecloth. When cold, it may be covered with glaze, as the *prensado de carne* (given above), or it may be sliced without the glaze, each slice placed on a slice of tomato, with a slice of stuffed olive on the top of each for garnish. Serves 10 to 12 as an appetizer.

ALCACHOFAS CON JAMON (Artichokes with Ham)

2 packages frozen artichoke
    hearts
1/2 cup Spanish olive oil
1/4 cup minced ham

2 slices onion
1/2 lemon, sliced
1/2 teaspoon salt

Place frozen artichoke hearts in heavy saucepan with the olive oil and salt, cover, heat until frozen blocks can be broken up. Add ham and onion, place lemon slices over top, cover again, cook until artichokes are tender. Serve artichokes either hot or cold, in their own sauce. Strips of pimiento may be added for color, if desired.

ENSALADA DE ALCACHOFAS (Artichoke Salad)

Cook frozen artichoke hearts in olive oil or water (I find they have much more flavor if cooked in oil). When cold, cover with the following sauce and marinate several hours.

SAUCE

½ cup olive oil	1 small onion, thinly sliced
2 tablespoons vinegar	2 tablespoons capers
Juice and grated rind ½ lemon	¼ teaspoon salt, or to taste
1 clove garlic, crushed	Pinch of cayenne pepper

Remove artichoke hearts from marinade, arrange on lettuce with quarters of tomatoes, hard-cooked eggs in wedges, and raw cauliflower thinly sliced. Sprinkle some of the sauce over the other salad ingredients.

Note: Shrimp marinated in this same sauce is superb.

PESCADO ESCABECHE (Pickled Fish)

1 pound small fish, such as smelt, or 1 pound sea bass, filleted	2 garlic cloves, peeled
	½ cup vinegar
	1 teaspoon paprika
1 tablespoon flour	1 bay leaf
¼ teaspoon salt	10 whole peppercorns
½ cup olive oil	1 jar (8 ounces) stuffed green olives, sliced
2 or 3 onions, sliced	
2 green peppers, sliced	

If sea bass is used, cut in long strips. Combine flour and salt, dust fish with mixture, then lightly brown in hot olive oil. Sauté fish only until golden, do not thoroughly cook. Remove from oil; drain on absorbent paper. To same oil add onions, sliced peppers, and the whole garlic cloves. Cook until limp; these should not be thoroughly cooked either. Discard garlic. Arrange a layer of the fish in a glass dish or deep crock, cover with a layer of the partially cooked onions and peppers, then a layer of the sliced olives. Repeat until all these ingredients have been used. To oil in pan add the vinegar, paprika, bay leaf, and peppercorns. Heat to boiling, pour over fish. Add vinegar enough to cover fish completely. Cover dish, place in refrigerator, leave several days. To serve, remove fish from marinade, arrange over lettuce.

PIMIENTOS FRITOS (Fried Pimientos)

Drain canned pimientos, cut in 2-inch squares, sauté in olive oil with 2 or 3 peeled cloves of garlic until delicately browned. Remove and discard garlic; sprinkle pimientos with salt. Serve hot or cold, sprinkled with minced fresh parsley. (Fresh red sweet peppers can be cooked the same way.)

In addition to the preceding, other *entremeses* may include several kinds of spicy sausages, usually thinly sliced, sautéed mushrooms filled with savory stuffings, oysters prettily served in the shell on fig leaves in woven baskets, caviar (Spanish caviar, from sturgeon which sometimes appear at the mouth of the Guadalquivir River), marinated cold trout, cold rice salad, small pieces of *bacalao* (salt cod) in a savory sauce, potato chips (exactly like ours, but fried in olive oil, which gives them a slightly different flavor), and *fiambres*, which can mean almost any kind of cold meat. But whatever else is offered, for true Spanish *tapas* be sure to include green olives and salted almonds—and sherry.

CHAPTER 3

Sopas

(SOUPS)

Almost overnight *gazpacho*, the salad-soup of Spain, has become an American food fashion. Yet whether gazpacho is really a soup at all is open to question. And in the northern provinces of Spain itself this wonderfully refreshing summer iced soup was scarcely known until recent years.

Gazpacho had its international following long ago, however. When thumbing through a copy of Mrs. Mary Randolph's *The Virginia Housewife*, one of the first of our American cookbooks, published originally in 1824, I came across a recipe for Spanish gazpacho made much as we make it today. And in 1840 the French writer Théophile Gautier wrote about having gazpacho during a trip through southern Spain. He asserted it would "have made the hair of Brillat-Savarin stand on end," though he concluded, "Strange as it may seem the first time one tastes it, one ends by getting used to it and even liking it."

Like most very old dishes, gazpacho recipes are multitudinous and each one different.

The peasant way of making gazpacho, everyone seems to agree, is to mash the tomatoes and other ingredients patiently and tirelessly in a huge wooden bowl, using a wooden pestle. This for example, is a peasant recipe for *gazpacho sevillano*:

"You must have a large wooden bowl, made from the trunk of a tree, gently hollowed in the center. In this bowl place some salt, quite a lot of garlic, and a little green pepper. With a pestle, pound thoroughly until the mixture is a smooth paste. Then add stale bread which has been grated into crumbs—the bread should be five or six days old. Pound the crumbs gradually into the vegetable mixture until again you have a smooth paste. Then you begin adding nice ripe tomatoes which have been peeled and seeded, and continue pounding and mashing until the mixture is thin, without any lumps. To this you add the yolk of a hard-cooked egg, blend thoroughly, and stir in olive oil—plenty of olive oil. Finally you add a little vinegar and enough water to make it the right consistency."

In Jerez, Anne Williams de Domecq (whose husband is director of the Williams & Humbert bodegas) told me that *gazpacho andaluz* (see below) should always be made with *sherry* vinegar. Jean Dalrymple of the New York City Center, who spent some twenty summers in the Valencia area of Spain when José Iturbi was one of her clients, learned to make a *gazpacho valenciana* from Señora Iturbi. Her version, Miss Dalrymple says, always included a pinch of cumin—a most important addition—along with garlic, fresh tomatoes, olive oil, and vinegar, and croutons of bread fried in olive oil served over the top as garnish.

In old cookbooks I found other gazpacho recipes which called for such diverse ingredients as toasted almonds, black and/or green olives, chicken broth instead of water, and even red wine. Minced cucumber or onions are very often served floating over the top. Pimientos or paprika in large amounts very frequently will be added. Sometimes other vegetables are puréed along with the tomatoes. There was even in one Spanish book a recipe for "*gazpacho colorado*" (literally red gazpacho), which turned out to be a thick *hot* purée served with big chunks of bread.

In all these different versions, four ingredients appear without fail: tomatoes, garlic, olive oil, and vinegar. The tomatoes must be fresh and sweet, preferably picked from the vine while still warm with the sun and rushed to the kitchen to be scalded, skins peeled off and the seeds extracted at once. In order to make a perfect gazpacho, the tomato seeds should be removed, for these do add a certain bitterness if left in. After the tomatoes have been puréed, they can be forced through a sieve to get rid of seeds. For those who do not have kitchen gardens, or who wish to make gazpacho before the local tomato season has reached its peak, it is best to use canned tomatoes, preferably the Italian pomodoro variety, or a very fine quality tomato purée.

The olive oil, of course, must be the very best. The amount of garlic used depends on personal taste and in general I would advise using less than Spanish cooks call for.

The elimination of bread from gazpacho takes it completely out of the peasant class, where it originated. The following versions of this cold Spanish soup are all made with an electric blender. I learned that even in Spain today those who have electric mixers or blenders make gazpacho this quicker, easier way.

GAZPACHO SEVILLANO

2 garlic cloves, minced
1 teaspoon salt
1 whole pimiento (from can)
¼ cup olive oil
¼ cup fine dry crumbs

8 large, ripe, local tomatoes,
  or 1 large can (1 pound 14
  ounces) best quality peeled
  tomatoes
2 tablespoons vinegar
Water as needed
Yolk of 1 hard-cooked egg
3 scallions, minced

Mash the garlic cloves with salt to a paste; add the pimiento, mash again to a paste. (A mortar and pestle are essential in a Spanish kitchen.) Work in the olive oil and bread crumbs. If fresh tomatoes are used, scald quickly with boiling water, peel off skins, quarter, and purée in electric blender. Force through sieve to remove seeds. If canned tomatoes are used, simply force through sieve. Combine with garlic paste and vinegar, return to blender, beat until thick and smooth. Chill thoroughly. When ready to serve, add ice-cold water (about 3 cups), and add more salt if needed. Pass sieved egg yolk and minced scallions as garnish. Makes 8 to 10 servings.

GAZPACHO VALENCIANA (Jean Dalrymple's Version)

2 cloves garlic, mashed
1 teaspoon salt
¼ teaspoon cumin
¼ cup Spanish olive oil
2 cups canned tomato purée,
  or 8 large sun-ripened tomatoes, peeled, seeded, and
  puréed

1 tablespoon vinegar
1 cup small bread cubes
Olive oil for frying
12 ice cubes
½ cucumber, minced
1 sweet red or green pepper,
  minced
2 scallions, minced

Crush garlic with salt and cumin, beat in olive oil, then combine with puréed tomatoes and vinegar. Beat in blender until smooth. Chill thoroughly. Sauté bread cubes in olive oil until crisp. Add ice cubes to chilled purée ½ hour before serving. Serve the sautéed croutons and the minced vegetables in separate bowls to add to the soup as garnish. Serves 6.

Note: Puréed tomatoes are *not* the same as tomato paste. If puréed tomatoes are not available, strain canned tomatoes carefully, beating to a purée in blender.

GAZPACHO ANDALUZ (Sophisticated Version)

8 large ripe tomatoes, peeled
and seeded, or large can
(1 pound 14 ounces) best
quality peeled tomatoes
2 or 3 garlic cloves, minced
1 teaspoon salt
1 tablespoon paprika
1 teaspoon sugar

1 cucumber, peeled and
chopped
Dash of cayenne or Tabasco
3 tablespoons olive oil
1 tablespoon vinegar
3 cups clear chicken broth
6 scallions, chopped
½ green pepper, minced

Mash garlic cloves, blend with salt, paprika and sugar; combine with cucumber, tomatoes, cayenne, olive oil, and vinegar. Beat in blender until smooth and thick. Chill thoroughly. When ready to serve, combine with chicken broth. Garnish with minced scallions and green pepper. Serve an ice cube in each soup plate. Chopped pitted black olives may also be served as garnish if desired.

*   *   *

Soup is an important part of every Spanish dinner—in fact, it would be unthinkable in Spain to have an evening meal without it. The soup may be simply bouillon sparked with sherry, or it may be a thick, hearty fish soup, or a well-seasoned broth in which eggs float plump and soft.

CONSOME SENCILLO (Clear Consommé)

1 quart (4 cups) beef bouillon
¼ cup amontillado sherry
1 teaspoon minced parsley

Most Americans will make bouillon the easy way, by opening a can or two, or by dissolving bouillon cubes or powder or liquid concentrate in boiling water. Even this short-cut consommé is delicious when Spanish sherry is added just before serving, and the bit of parsley on top also contributes delightful flavor. But for the more ambitious, a far richer bouillon is made by simmering bones and vegetables 3 or 4 hours in salted water; or use a pressure cooker and have the job finished in 25 minutes. For a quart of water, use a pound of bones, preferably one veal knuckle and some beef neck bones, 2 quartered onions, a cubed carrot, and 2 stalks of celery. Simmer uncovered over heat so low that liquid just "smiles"; or cook under 15 pounds of pressure, letting liquid cool in pot. When cool, strain, let strained liquid chill in refrigerator, then scrape fat and scum from jellied stock. It's really quite easy—try it sometime, and you'll be surprised. One quart of bouillon serves 8.

SOPA REAL (Royal Soup)

Buy the smallest-size can of boned chicken and chop meat into tiny pieces. Combine with ½ cup minced cooked ham (leftover from roast), 2 hard-cooked eggs, chopped, and 4 cups bouillon made with bouillon cubes or powder. Bring to a boil, simmer gently about 3 minutes, add ¼ cup sherry. Serve to 8, with a few croutons over each serving. (To make croutons, chop white bread into small cubes, sauté in olive oil or a blend of olive oil and melted butter until golden.)

CONSOME MADRILENO (Spanish Onion Soup)

2 *large Spanish Onions, or 4*	⅛ *teaspoon mace*
medium yellow onions	⅛ *teaspoon powdered cloves*
1 *cup olive oil*	1 *teaspoon vinegar*
2 *teaspoons salt*	2 *tablespoons minced parsley*
6 *cups boiling water*	6 *eggs*
¼ *teaspoon black pepper*	6 *slices toast*

Simmer sliced onions in olive oil until very soft; do not allow to brown. Add salt, water, spices and vinegar, bring to a boil, lower heat, simmer 15 minutes. Break the eggs one at a time into a saucer, carefully slide the eggs into the broth, cook gently until eggs are firm. Sprinkle parsley over top. Meantime, toast the bread, lay a slice of toast in each of 6 soup plates, remove poached eggs from soup with slotted spoon and place on toast. Cover eggs with soup. Makes 6 generous servings.

* * *

Nothing is more characteristic of Spain than its garlic soup, *sopa de ajo* (see below). In its simplest form, this is nothing more than garlic, oil, bread and water, a broth with little nourishment and little flavor—except that of the all-persuasive garlic. It has served to keep many a Spanish family from starvation, however, and in the rugged mountainous areas of the country, starvation is often a serious threat, especially during the winter months.

The more complex versions of garlic soup can be quite good —though one must like garlic, of course. The first of the two that follow is enriched with tomato, chicken broth, and eggs. The second, a version served in Málaga, may be iced, with grapes or melons added to it. Iced garlic soup may sound utterly awful, but it is not. Thanks to the addition of almonds, chicken broth, and the melon, this is quite a delicious concoction. Málaga is the southernmost city of Spain and it never freezes there, not even in midwinter. In the summer months, the temperature often goes over 100°. There are beaches all over, wonderful beaches, and there are moutainside retreats where cooling breezes may be enjoyed. On a clear day, it is possible to see the peaks of Africa across the Mediterranean from Málaga, especially if one is dining high on the hill known as Gibralfaro, once the site of a Moorish fortress (and before that a Roman, and even earlier an Iberian fortress). To sip at an iced garlic soup containing almonds and melons in such an exotic setting seems not strange at all.

SOPA DE AJO (Hot Garlic Soup)

6 garlic cloves	½ bay leaf, crushed
6 slices bread, cubed	1 teaspoon paprika
3 tablespoons olive oil	3 cups chicken broth
1 medium can (1 pound)	Salt to taste
tomatoes, sieved	6 eggs
	Minced parsley for garnish

Place whole peeled garlic cloves and cubes of bread in hot oil, sauté until golden. Remove garlic and discard; remove the bread, mash to a paste. (If a strong garlic flavor is desired, mash the garlic and bread together.) To crushed bread, add sieved tomatoes, bay leaf, paprika, and chicken broth. Simmer 15 minutes. Salt to taste. Separate the eggs, add some of the hot broth to egg yolks, then add egg yolks to remaining broth, beating until smooth. Do the same with the unbeaten egg whites, beating quickly to blend thoroughly. Sprinkle minced parsley over top and serve at once. Serves 6.

Variation: Poach the eggs in the hot broth as for the consommé madrileño.

SOPA DE AJO BLANCO (Cold Garlic Soup with Melon or Grapes)

3 or 4 garlic cloves
10 almonds, blanched, toasted
2 tablespoons olive oil
2 slices white bread, in small cubes
1 teaspoon salt
Dash of pepper

3 cups clear chicken broth
½ tablespoon wine vinegar, or
2 tablespoons very dry white wine
1 cup cubed melon or seeded white grapes
6 ice cubes

Crush garlic, removing all bits of skin. Crush almonds in electric blender or with mortar and pestle. Mix almonds and garlic with olive oil and bread crumbs, sauté until bread is golden. Mash to a paste, add salt and pepper, chicken broth, vinegar or wine, and fruit. Chill thoroughly. Serve to 6 persons, with an ice cube in each plate.

Another soup I enjoyed while in Málaga was one listed on menus as *sopa de viña* A.B. When I tried to learn the meaning of the name, I was told that it referred to the sherry used in making the soup. However, in other parts of Spain I encountered a similar soup called *sopa malagueña*—soup of Málaga —which seems an easier name.

SOPA MALAGUENA (Seafood Soup of Málaga)

½ pound very small shrimp
1 pound white-fleshed fish— haddock, hake, turbot
6 cups fish stock

2 tablespoons dry sherry
½ cup peas (fresh or frozen)
1 egg yolk
1 tablespoon heavy cream
Minced parsley

Shell the shrimp, saving shells for making the fish stock. Have fish filleted and use bones and head or tail of fish for the stock too: add these to 7 cups water with 1 medium onion, quartered, 2 whole cloves, ½ teaspoon bouquet of herbs and

1 teaspoon salt (or to taste). Bring to a boil, cook 20 minutes; reducing to 6 cups; strain, saving clear stock. Combine the stock with sherry, add peas and the fish cut into 2-inch square pieces, bring again to a boil, cook over low heat 10 minutes. Add shrimp, cook 4 minutes longer. Beat the egg yolk, add a little of the hot broth, then combine with remaining broth. Cook over very low heat until broth is thickened. Add cream. Serve sprinkled with minced parsley. Makes 8 to 10 servings.

A very popular soup, one found on many restaurant menus, is *sopa de cuarto de hora*, though the name is deceptive, for considerably more than a quarter of an hour is required in its preparation. It is delicious, nevertheless, and for us hearty enough for a luncheon soup, though for the Spanish it seems to serve only as a first course for dinner.

SOPA DE CUARTO DE HORA (Quarter-of-an-Hour Soup)

2 to 3 tablespoons Spanish olive oil
1 medium onion, chopped fine
¼ pound ham, finely diced
¼ pound shelled shrimp
¼ cup blanched almonds, ground fine

1 ripe tomato, peeled and chopped, or ½ tablespoon tomato paste
6 cups clear consommé
1 cup uncooked rice
2 cans (7½ ounces) minced clams and liquid
2 hard-cooked eggs, minced
½ cup shelled green peas

Sauté onion in olive oil until tender but not brown; push to one side, add ham, shrimp, and almonds, cook until ham is lightly browned and shrimp bright pink. Remove shrimp, chop fine. Add ripe tomato or paste to ham, cook until soft and well blended. Add consommé and minced clams, bring to a boil. When rapidly boiling, add rice, lower heat, simmer 20 minutes or until tender. During last 10 minutes add peas (if frozen, in last 5 minutes). Just before serving, replace shrimp. Serve soup in individual casseroles garnished with minced egg. Makes 6 to 8 servings.

There are many wonderful fish soups in Spain, differing from province to province. A superb but rather complicated one is the following *guisado de pescados*, which is served at the Castellana Hilton Hotel in Madrid. In San Sebastián I enjoyed a most wonderful *crema de mariscos* at the elegant old restaurant Casa Nicolasa. These cannot be compared to the bouillabaisse of France, for they are completely different, but, like bouillabaisse, they are extraordinary enough to be served as the *pièce de résistance* for a supper and to be remembered long after as gourmet treasures.

GUISADO DE PESCADOS (Fish Soup)

½ cup olive oil
2 medium onions, minced
3 garlic cloves, minced
3 peeled, chopped tomatoes, or 1 medium can (1 pound) tomatoes
2 quarts fish stock
½ pound shrimp in shell
1 teaspoon salt
Pinch of saffron
2 leeks or 6 scallions, sliced
2 carrots, thinly sliced

1 pound cod, haddock, or halibut, cut in serving pieces
½ pound scallops
3 rock lobster tails, cut in thirds
4 small fish, red mullet or butterfish, cut in serving pieces
⅓ cup dry white wine
⅓ cup dry anise liqueur (or Pernod)
Fried croutons

Sauté onions and garlic in half the olive oil; add tomato, cook until well blended. Make a fish stock meantime by cooking heads and tails of fish and the shrimp shells in 2 quarts water with 1 teaspoon salt and the saffron for 20 to 30 minutes; strain. Add strained stock to onions along with leeks, and carrots. Boil hard 10 minutes. Separately in remaining ¼ cup olive oil sauté the fish, scallops, lobster, and small fish until lobster shells are bright red and fish golden; add shrimp, cook until faintly pink. Add fish and shellfish, wine and anise to tomato mixture, cook 5 minutes. Remove fish and shellfish to be served as the entree, with Spanish mayonnaise (see Index) as the sauce. Serve the broth as a first course, each serving topped with fried croutons (small cubes of bread fried until golden in olive oil or blended olive oil and butter). Serves 10.

Note: If neither anise nor Pernod is handy or available, add ¼ teaspoon powdered anise (the herb) or fennel to the fish stock.

CREMA DE MARISCOS (Shellfish Bisque)

3 *pounds (about) fish heads and tails*	3 *stalks celery, chopped*
½ *pound small raw shrimp in shell*	1 *large can (1 pound 14 ounces) best quality tomatoes*
1 *sea bass*	½ *teaspoon thyme*
1 *can crab meat*	½ *teaspoon saffron*
1 *lobster tail, raw*	1 *bay leaf*
6 *tablespoons olive oil*	¼ *cup minced parsley*
2 *garlic cloves, crushed*	1 *cup dry white wine*
3 *leeks, chopped*	2 *cups water*
1 *medium onion, chopped*	2 *teaspoons salt, or to taste*

Sauté the garlic, leeks, onion, and celery in the olive oil until soft. Remove vegetables to large kettle. Cook the sea bass in the olive oil until golden; separate fish meat from bones and set it aside. Add bones, head, and tail to kettle. Shell shrimp, remove shell from lobster tail, put lobster meat and shelled shrimp aside. Add shells of shrimp and lobster to kettle, along with tomatoes, herbs, wine, water and salt. Bring to a boil, boil hard 20 minutes. Remove fish bones and shrimp shells with slotted spoon; force remainder through sieve. It should be a smooth purée, the consistency of heavy cream. Add more liquid if too thick. Replace fish in this purée along with the minced raw shrimp, the chopped lobster meat (raw), and the crab meat, with all gristle removed. Bring to a boil, cook 3 or 4 minutes. Taste for seasoning, adjust if needed. Makes 6 to 8 servings.

Catalonia, on Spain's northeast coast, has a cuisine much like that of Provence. Here is a simple vegetable soup that is delicious. The bouillon can be made with powdered concentrate or cubes, or with canned concentrated bouillon, but naturally well-flavored homemade meat stock is preferable.

SOPA DE CATALONIA (Catalan Vegetable Soup)

2 onions, chopped
2 leeks, white part only, chopped
1 tablespoon olive oil
1 tablespoon sweet butter
1 stalk celery, minced

3 ripe tomatoes, peeled, diced
2 medium potatoes, raw, diced
⅓ cup dry white wine
6 cups beef bouillon
1 teaspoon minced parsley

Cook onions and leeks in olive oil and butter until onion is soft; add celery and tomatoes, cook until tomato is reduced and very soft; add potatoes, wine, and bouillon, cook 30 minutes or until potatoes are very soft. Serve this way or purée in an electric blender. Serve topped with minced parsley. Makes 8 servings.

Garbanzos—chick-peas—are used by the Spanish in many ways and all are delicious. However, my attempts to re-create these Spanish recipes with our supermarket chick-peas have been disappointing, apparently because the peas themselves simply do not have as much flavor as those in Spain. I have tried both the dried peas and the canned chick-peas; of the two the canned peas are preferable. One brand, Mare Chiaro is almost as nutty in flavor as the Spanish garbanzos. Perhaps those who live in an area where there are many Americans of Spanish descent or Latin Americans will be able to find dried garbanzos that are more like those in Spain; if so, I can heartily recommend this *potaje de garbanzos*. Incidentally, the same recipe can be used with little white navy beans or with lentils instead of garbanzos with delicious results. Do *not* soak the peas or beans overnight—it is not necessary, and much flavor is lost.

POTAJE DE GARBANZOS (Chick-Pea Soup)

1 pound dried chick-peas	2 tomatoes, peeled and
1 cup olive oil	chopped
2 medium onions, sliced	3 quarts water
1 carrot, diced	1 teaspoon minced parsley
2 to 4 garlic cloves, crushed	½ bay leaf, crushed
¼ pound cooked ham, minced	Salt to taste
½ pound chorizo sausage	¼ teaspoon black pepper
(flavored with garlic and	
paprika)	

Cover peas with water, bring to a boil, drain and discard water. Meantime, cook vegetables, ham, and sausage in olive oil until onion is tender. Add the chick-peas, 3 quarts water, and herbs and season the liquid to taste. Simmer 3 hours or until peas are tender. Serve this way or force through sieve or food mill to serve as a purée. Makes 4 to 6 hearty servings.

Variation: Either navy beans or lentils may be used in the above, but the cooking time will be shorter, probably no more than 2 hours.

The following is a recipe for a bean soup or stew from north Spain, the region of Galicia, where salt pork or lard is used rather than olive oil. This, again, is a matter of both economics and geography. Not many olive trees grow in Galicia, but

nearly every peasant family raises its own pigs. Lard is cheaper
for them than olive oil, so their bean soup takes on a different
flavor.

CALDO GALLEGO (Soup of Galicia)

½ pound dried chick-peas or
white beans
¼ pound lean salt pork
¼ cup chopped cooked ham
¼ pound chorizo sausage,
sliced
2 tomatoes, peeled and
chopped

2 garlic cloves, minced
1 ham bone
2 quarts water
Salt to taste
4 to 6 small white potatoes,
peeled and chopped
½ pound spinach

Cover peas or beans with water, bring to a boil, discard water. Draw out fat from salt pork in heavy pot or skillet; add
ham and sausage, cook until lightly browned. Add tomatoes
and garlic, cook about 2 minutes. Add chick-peas or beans, the
ham bone, water, and salt. Cover, bring to a boil, cook three
hours. During last half hour, add potatoes, chopped in small
dice. During last 5 minutes add spinach, which has been
thoroughly washed and chopped.

* * *

In the city of Segovia, north of Madrid, there is a famous
restaurant called Mesón de Cándido, which has stood on the
same spot, run by members of the same family, for seven
hundred years. This is a fascinating place to visit, because the
restaurant is in the shadow of a giant Roman aqueduct which
towers ninety feet above the town, stretching for ten miles between hills. On the hilltop just above the restaurant stands
the famous alcazar of Segovia, a Moorish palace-fortress taken
over by the Castilians when Isabella and Ferdinand came to

power. Its turrets arise in fragile beauty on a peak with sharply sloping sides.

The following soup, served regularly on the menu at Mesón de Cándido, has been a specialty of the house since the fourteenth century. This is truly Spanish!

SOPA CASTELLANA SIGLO XIV
(Soup in 14th-Century-Castilian Style)

¼ cup olive oil	1 small onion, minced
3 slices bread, crust removed	1 teaspoon paprika
4 ounces ham, minced (½ cup)	4 cups beef or chicken broth
2 garlic cloves, minced	6 eggs

Break the bread into crumbs, sauté with the ham, garlic, and onion in oil over moderate heat until onion is tender (do not allow to brown). Add paprika and slowly add broth. (Excellent broth is easy to make with marrow bones, which your butcher will often give you free on request, or with chicken necks and backs. Cover with 5 cups water, add an onion, 2 cloves, 1 teaspoon salt, and ¼ teaspoon herbs. Cover, cook ½ hour, strain.) Simmer soup 10 minutes after adding broth; taste for seasoning—it may need more salt. Turn boiling soup into 6 individual casseroles. Break an egg into each. Place in preheated 400° oven until eggs are set, about 10 minutes. Yolks should be soft, white just firm. Serves 6.

CHAPTER 4

Huevos

(EGGS)

In Spain the egg always comes first. Spanish hens must be incredibly prolific, because more eggs seemed to be consumed in Spain, in more diverse and ingenious ways, than in any other corner of the world. Out of curiosity once I counted the number of dishes listed under *Huevos* on a menu—this was in Málaga, as I remember. The total was thirty-six. Hard-cooked eggs appear cold with the *entremeses*, jellied, or stuffed. Soft-cooked eggs are even rolled in crumbs and deep-fried to be eaten like fritters. As a first course, eggs may be brought to you in little individual ramekins, baked with ham, with asparagus, blanketed with a cheese sauce, simmered in tomato sauce, nested with grilled kidneys, or perched over fresh sardines. Or as tortillas.

Tortilla is the Spanish name for omelet, but the omelets of Spain are a law unto themselves. They are fat and hearty, full of all sorts of things, such as minced brains, chicken livers, a medley of vegetables, or chopped-up bits of seafood. The way of making a Spanish omelet is unique too. I have attempted to describe the method as clearly as possible in the following tortilla recipes, but, quite frankly, it is a trick to be learned, requiring more dexterity than a simple French omelet. Mind you, I'm not downgrading the omelets of France. I simply mean that it takes a special kind of skill to turn out a thick Spanish omelet in one piece. But do try it. For us, these make wonderful luncheon or Sunday supper dishes—and you may use up any bits of leftovers you happen to have in the refrigerator or on the pantry shelf. The simple Spanish omelet, the kind encountered most frequently, is made with nothing but potatoes and eggs (or potatoes, *onions*, and eggs). And *very important*: always use olive oil. Olive oil will not stick to the pan. Other oils or fats will. If you insist on butter, use a combination of butter and olive oil.

The use of eggs does not end with the *huevos* course. They are used in all sorts of sauces and in intricate desserts. In this chapter, however, only the ways of using eggs for first course or main course dishes are included.

HUEVOS AL PLATO (Eggs in Ramekins)

This is the Spanish version of the French *oeufs au plat*, but how different! The following is typical. You may find it done in a dozen different ways in Spanish restaurants, but nearly always onions and olive oil are included in some manner. You must have shallow individual ramekins—deep casseroles will not do.

1 small onion, minced   4 eggs
¼ cup chopped ham   Salt and pepper
2 tablespoons olive oil or 1
   tablespoon each butter and
   oil

Cook onion and ham in olive oil (or oil and butter) until onion is tender; sprinkle lightly with salt and pepper. Transfer to 2 individual ramekins (dividing equally). Break 2 eggs in each ramekin. Sprinkle a little salt and pepper over top of eggs. Bake in oven preheated to 400° for 10 minutes or until whites of eggs are just set. For 2 persons.

HUEVOS REVUELTOS CON TOMATE
(Scrambled Eggs with Tomato)

Sauté a peeled, chopped tomato and a little minced onion (about 1 tablespoonful) in butter until onion is tender. Sprinkle with a little salt from shaker. Add ¼ teaspoon salt to 2 or 3 well-beaten eggs, stir to blend, add to tomato in pan, lift up with spatula lightly as egg firms, folding over continuously. Makes 2 servings.

Variation: omit onion, add 1 teaspoon minced parsley and a pinch of sugar to tomato.

HUEVOS BÉCHAMEL (Eggs in White Sauce)

Soft-boil eggs in the shell gently (3½ minutes in boiling water). Drain off hot water, add cold water, quickly remove shells, leaving eggs whole. Place eggs on a bed of rice (2 eggs for each serving) or on a bed of fine noodles. Cover with *béchamel* sauce (white sauce flavored with nutmeg), sprinkle grated Parmesan or other dry, mild cheese over top. Place briefly under broiler (4 inches from heat) to glaze. Serve as first course or luncheon entree.

HUEVOS REVUELTOS CON CHAMPINONES
(Scrambled Eggs with Mushrooms)

Sauté a few thin-sliced mushrooms in butter until lightly browned. Beat 1 or 2 eggs with fork, lightly, add a pinch of salt, freshly ground pepper, and a tablespoon of water or cream (not milk). Add to the pan with the mushrooms, gently lift up and fold over with spatula as egg firms. For 1 serving.

* * *

Other ways of serving scrambled eggs in Spain: brown sliced *chorizo* (sausage flavored with paprika and garlic) in olive oil before adding eggs; or brown ham in butter; or cook sliced kidneys or chicken livers in butter until browned; or add to the beaten eggs (before pouring into pan) cooked peas, diced pimiento, beans, or diced asparagus. Or add just about any bits and pieces of things you find in the refrigerator.

* * *

HUEVOS A LA CUBANA

Considering the close ties between Spain and Latin America, both culturally and economically, it is surprising that so few Latin-American dishes have found favor in Spain. This way of preparing eggs, however, is popular nearly everywhere —especially so in Andalusia and Barcelona.

Fry 1 or 2 eggs (for each serving) gently in olive oil, sprinkling lightly with salt (or poach eggs in acidulated water, if preferred). Place eggs over a mound of hot cooked rice. Eggs sometimes are accompanied by fried ripe bananas, sometimes served with tomato sauce. Amazingly good: the soft egg yolk, blended with the rice, has rich flavor.

* * *

Huevos a la flamenca have become as close to a national dish as *paella:* you find it offered on virtually every restaurant menu, in every city of Spain, though it originated in Andalusia, home of the flamenco dance. The Spanish order it as a first course; for us it is an entree. A good spur-of-the-moment dish for company.

HUEVOS A LA FLAMENCA (Eggs Flamenco)

8 eggs
2 tablespoons olive oil
1 small garlic clove, minced
1 large onion, sliced or
   chopped
½ pound chorizo, sliced, or 1
   cup diced cooked ham
1 teaspoon minced parsley

2 canned pimientos, diced
2 tomatoes, peeled and
   chopped
¼ teaspoon salt
½ cup clear chicken broth
1 cup cooked peas
8 cooked or canned asparagus
   spears

Sauté onion and garlic in olive oil until tender; add sausage, cut in slices, or ham, cook until lightly browned. Add parsley and diced pimientos; cook about 2 minutes. Add tomatoes, salt, and chicken broth, simmer until sauce is well blended. Divide sauce in four parts, pour into 4 shallow ramekins. Break two eggs into each. Arrange cooked peas and asparagus around eggs, pushing down into sauce. Bake in preheated 350° oven until eggs are just set, about 20 minutes. Serve at once. Makes 4 servings.

HUEVOS CON BERENJENAS (Eggs with Eggplant)

Sauté 1 cup chopped eggplant in olive oil with 1 small chopped onion and 1 crushed garlic clove until vegetables are tender, about 15 minutes. Add 1 peeled, chopped tomato, cook a few minutes longer. Add salt and pepper to taste. Transfer to 2 individual casseroles. Break an egg into each. Place in oven preheated to 400° F., bake until egg is just set, about 15 minutes. Makes 2 servings.

HUEVOS A LA RIOJANA (Eggs Rioja Style)

These are eggs baked in a simple tomato sauce—the classic Spanish tomato sauce, made of olive oil, onion, garlic, pimiento, tomato, and herbs. For a short cut use an 8-ounce can of tomato sauce, add ⅓ cup olive oil, ¼ teaspoon instant minced garlic, 1 teaspoon of instant minced onion, and a well-drained, chopped pimiento. Simmer about 5 minutes, divide into 4 individual ramekins. Break 1 or 2 eggs into each, bake in a preheated 400° oven for 12 to 15 minutes until eggs are just firm. 4 servings.

HUEVOS A LA ZINGARA (Eggs Gypsy Style)

1 tablespoon olive oil
2 strips bacon, diced
1 small onion, chopped
½ green pepper, minced
1 or 2 garlic cloves, minced
1 teaspoon tomato catsup
1 tablespoon dry sherry
½ cup beef bouillon
4 eggs

Cook onion and bacon in olive oil until bacon is crisp; add garlic and green pepper, cook about 1 minute, add catsup, sherry, and bouillon. Simmer 5 minutes. Divide into 2 individual casseroles or ramekins. Break 2 eggs into each. Bake in preheated 350° oven until eggs are just set, about 15 minutes. 2 servings.

CAZUELA DE HABAS A LA GRANADINA
(Lima-Bean Casserole Granada Style)

2 onions, chopped
2 garlic cloves, minced
¼ cup olive oil
¼ cup tomato sauce
1 package frozen baby Limas
⅛ teaspoon crushed dried mint
½ teaspoon minced fresh parsley
¼ teaspoon saffron (optional)
¼ teaspoon cumin
½ cup beef bouillon
4 to 6 eggs

Cook onions and garlic in the olive oil until soft, add tomato sauce, Limas (still frozen). Dissolve leaf saffron in 2 tablespoons boiling water, strain, add strained liquid with herbs, spices, and bouillon to beans. Cook covered until beans are tender, stirring once or twice to break up block. Transfer to shallow casserole. Break eggs over beans. Bake in oven preheated to 350° until whites are firm, about 15 minutes. Serves 3 to 4. (Tiny *habas*, the Spanish broad beans, are used in Granada. Our baby Limas give a completely different flavor, but they are the closest we have.)

* * *

Granada was the last Moorish city lost to the Spaniards, and the place most beloved by them in all of Spain. To this day, there is so strong a Moorish influence in Granada one can almost imagine the ghosts of turbaned sultans lurking behind the high white walls. It is in Granada that the Alhambra stands, that startlingly beautiful palace with its poetic courtyards and whispering fountains which so inspired Washington Irving. The day I was in Granada, the English-speaking guide who escorted me through the Alhambra offered to walk with me through a typical street in the old quarter where, even on a Sunday morning, housewives were buying vegetables and fish and eggs from street vendors. Some of the food was piled right on the cobblestones of the street, guarded over by sly-looking men whose eyes crinkled in brown faces, some of them sitting on their haunches beside their wares. A burro came down the street, stepping over the piles of food, a basket filled with long loaves of bread perched high on his back, his long ears and sad eyes the ultimate in patience. Reaching a small square, we saw a woman making *churros*, the Spanish doughnuts. The churro women have long pastry guns which they fill with simple flour-and-yeast dough, then they squirt the dough into kettles of sizzling oil, where it forms enormous thin circles which bounce on the oil until golden. The guide bought one for me, the huge circle costing a single peseta, and I broke it in pieces to taste gingerly. It was delicious, crisp, nutlike, wonderfully fresh.

Finally we stopped into a small bar to have coffee, the bitter, strong coffee of Spain, scarcely able to hear one another above the raucous din; a juke box screeched the wailing native music of Andalusia, a big-bosomed woman at the coffee urn joked with loud laughter with the lank-haired men on the other side of the bar. As we went out again, the guide exclaimed, "It's just like Morocco—you might be in Tangier. It hasn't changed here for hundreds of years." Walking away, up narrow cobblestone paths with high walls on either side, he pointed to gates of houses set in the walls, saying that most of these houses had been here from the fourteenth century, looking much as they did now. We walked around the *carmen* (a Moorish word for a house with garden) where the composer De Falla once lived, where he wrote his immortal *Nights in the Gardens of Spain*. The guide told me of other world-renowned artists who had lived in Granada at various times, in a city whose university is one of the oldest in Europe. "Would you like to see where the gypsies live?" he asked. There are more gypsies in Granada than anywhere else in Spain, and of course I wanted to see these people who have been so romanticized in literature. This time we drove to the area where gypsy caves honeycomb a hillside—had we walked, he explained, they would not have left us alone for a moment. He knew them well, being a guide, and chose one of the more elaborate cave-homes for me to visit. I was surprised at its comfort: there were several rooms, divided by walls, with windows in each outside room and a small kitchen where a tiny gypsy woman was cooking a stew. The guide had only comtempt for the gypsies, however. "They are thieves, you can't trust one of them. They care for nothing but money—easy money. The girls marry at twelve, have three or four children by the time they are eighteen. They are shiftless and ignorant."

For lunch we went to a modest restaurant so that I might taste (as he put it) the kind of food the Spanish people eat rather than tourist fare. One of the dishes he chose was a *cazuela de habas.* The other was *tortilla al Sacromonte.* This omelet is named for the monastery where it was first created, by a monk whose love of good food was equaled by his sense of economy. It is made with bits of this and that, but always some calf's brain, a bit of tomato (not too much), usually some chicken livers, and perhaps a bit of bacon or ham. It was one of the most delicious omelets I have ever tasted.

TORTILLA AL SACROMONTE (Omelet Sacromonte)

1 *calf's brain*
3 *or 4 chicken livers*
1 *tablespoon minced onion*
2 *tablespoons minced ham*
2 *tablespoons olive oil*

1 *small tomato, peeled and chopped, or 1 tablespoon tomato catsup*
4 *eggs, beaten*
½ *teaspoon salt*

Cook calf's brain in 2 cups salted water and 2 tablespoons vinegar until firm and white, about 20 minutes. Drain and cool. Chop in small pieces. Cut chicken livers in quarters, sauté with onion and ham in olive oil; add tomato and ¼ teaspoon salt, cook 5 minutes longer; add chopped brain. Beat eggs until frothy; season with ¼ teaspoon salt. Add ⅓ of the eggs at a time to the mixture in the pan, lifting as the egg firms to allow the moist egg to run under. When all the egg has been added, and a golden crust is beginning to form on the bottom, place a plate over the pan, invert, slide out the omelet. Scrape any bits on the bottom of the pan, moisten with a little more olive oil, slide the omelet back in again, moist side down. Cook until egg is firm on bottom. Serves 2 persons.

* * *

Another dish from Granada is this unusual arrangement of a spicy spinach purée in nests, holding golden jewels of eggs. Like the *cazuela*, it has decided Moorish flavoring.

ESPINACAS Y HUEVOS A LA GRANADINA
(Spinach and Eggs Granada Style)

1 *pound spinach, washed,* *cooked, chopped*	2 *peppercorns*
20 *almonds, blanched, toasted*	2 *cumin seeds, or pinch of* *powdered cumin*
2 *tablespoons olive oil*	1 *cup bouillon (beef or* *chicken)*
2 *slices bread*	
1 *or 2 garlic cloves*	6 *eggs*
½ *teaspoon powdered saffron*	4 *ounces (½ cup) lean cooked* *ham*
1 *whole clove*	

Coarsely chop almonds (this can be done in electric blender), sauté in olive oil along with bread broken into small crumbs. Meantime, mash garlic in mortar, add saffron, whole clove, peppercorns, and cumin, mash to a paste. Add enough water to make a sauce the consistency of thick cream. Combine garlic paste with almonds and bread crumbs, then add to spinach with bouillon. Place in electric blender, beat until puréed. Divide spinach in 6 parts, make a nest of spinach purée in each of 6 individual ramekins, with a well in center of each. Break an egg into each nest. Cut ham in julienne strips, lay over the egg. Bake in preheated 400° oven until egg white has just set. Serves 6 persons.

* * *

This is the classic peasant omelet, the one most frequently served in Spain. Often it is served cold as an appetizer, and the nutty flavor of potatoes and onions cooked in olive oil makes it delicious even when chilled. This is totally unlike the "Spanish omelet" served in American restaurants; in fact tomato sauce with omelet is a rarity in Spain.

TORTILLA CON PATATAS (Potato Omelet)

1 *medium onion*	½ *teaspoon salt*
2 *medium potatoes*	4 *large or 5 medium eggs, well*
4 *to 6 tablespoons olive oil*	*beaten*

Chop both onion and peeled potatoes into tiny cubes. Cover bottom of 10-inch omelet pan or heavy skillet with the olive oil (an omelet pan with sloping sides is preferable), add the chopped onions and potatoes. Cook over very low heat until vegetables are tender, chopping with a sharp knife as they cook and turning occasionally with spatula to prevent sticking. Vegetables should not brown. When very tender, sprinkle salt over top, stir to mix salt through vegetables, and drain off excess olive oil. Add about a third of the beaten eggs to the pan, lifting up as omelet sets to allow moist egg to run under. When this part of egg is solid, add another third of the beaten egg, lifting in the same way; finally repeat with remaining egg. Keep heat as low as possible, using asbestos pad under pan if you cannot regulate heat low enough. When golden crust has formed, loosen omelet all around edge and underneath with spatula, invert plate over top of pan, then turn out upside down on plate. Clean out any bits sticking to the pan, rub with a bit more olive oil, then slide the omelet back again, moist side down. Cook as before until solid. Makes 4 servings.

TORTILLA DE CANGREJO (Crab-Meat Omelet)

1 *can (4½ ounces) crab meat*	1 *tablespoon olive oil, or half*
or shrimp, drained	*olive oil, half butter*
	4 *eggs*

Remove gristle from crab meat, put crab or shrimp through food grinder, or beat in electric blender, or mash with mortar and pestle. Blend with olive oil. Add eggs, beat to mix thoroughly. Heat about ½ tablespoon olive oil in an omelet pan (if a skillet is to be used, increase amount of oil), "rolling" pan so that oil covers every inch of bottom. Add egg mixture, cook over very low heat until golden crust is formed, lifting up with spatula as it cooks to allow moist egg to run under. Place plate over pan, invert omelet to slide out. Clean out any bits sticking to pan, add another half tablespoon of oil to pan, slide omelet back into pan with moist side on bottom. Continue to cook over lowest heat until bottom crust is golden. Serve with mayonnaise as sauce. May be garnished with pimiento-stuffed olives, thinly sliced radishes and cucumbers. Makes 2 to 4 servings. Serve immediately.

TORTILLA CON ESPARRAGOS (Asparagus Omelet)

8 stalks canned white aspara-   4 eggs
   gus, diced   Salt and pepper
1 tablespoon butter

Cook diced asparagus in butter just until heated through. Add eggs, which have been beaten until frothy, seasoned with salt and pepper. Lift up with spatula as egg firms, folding over continuously. When solid throughout, slip out on plate. Serves 2.

TORTILLA CON HABAS (Bean Omelet)

Sauté 1 medium onion in 2 tablespoons olive oil until soft, add 1 cup cooked Lima beans or fava beans and ¼ cup tomato sauce, cook about 2 minutes. Beat 4 eggs until frothy, season with ¼ teaspoon salt and a little pepper; add to bean mixture. Cook over very low heat until firm, lifting up with spatula around edges and chopping in center to allow moist egg to run under. When firm and lightly brown on bottom, flip out on plate (as for *tortilla con patatas,* given above), add a little more oil to pan, slide back in again. Cook until firm. Cut into wedges to serve. Makes 2 to 4 servings.

TORTILLA CON CALABACINES (Squash Omelet)

Cut 1 medium zucchini or small yellow summer squash into ¼-inch slices, sauté in olive oil until lightly browned on each side, sprinkling lightly with salt. Beat 3 or 4 eggs until frothy, adding a pinch of salt. Pour off any excess oil from pan, then add eggs, lifting up with spatula as the egg firms. When firm throughout, flip over on plate. 2 to 4 servings.

TORTILLA PRIMAVERA (Spring Omelet)

1 *medium tomato, peeled and chopped*
1 *small onion, chopped*
3 *tablespoons olive oil*
1 *pound fresh peas, shelled, cooked; or ½ package frozen peas, cooked*

8 *eggs, beaten until light*
½ *teaspoon salt*
3 *tablespoons grated mild cheese*

Cook tomato and onion in olive oil until soft and well blended; add peas, cook 30 seconds. Beat eggs with salt and cheese, add to vegetables: lift up with spatula as the egg firms on the bottom, letting the moist egg run under. When firm throughout, place plate over pan, invert, slide out. Add more oil to pan, return with moist side on bottom. Cook until firm throughout. A 10-inch omelet pan will be needed for this. An excellent choice for luncheon. Serve at once to 4 persons.

HUEVOS A LA SEVILLANA (Eggs Seville Style)

¼ *cup olive oil*
2 *slices white bread, in cubes*
1 *small onion, chopped*
1 *small tomato, peeled and chopped, or 1 tablespoon catsup*

1 *or 2 garlic cloves, minced*
½ *cup water*
½ *teaspoon salt*
1 *package frozen Fordhook Limas*
4 *to 6 eggs*
8 *stalks green asparagus*

Sauté bread cubes in the olive oil; transfer to shallow casserole (a 10-inch round or square baking dish 1 inch deep is perfect). Add onion to skillet, tomato (or catsup), and garlic, cook until onion is soft. Add water, salt, and beans, cook until beans are tender. Transfer beans and tomato mixture to casserole, placing over bread. Break eggs over the beans. Arrange asparagus stalks around the eggs. Bake in preheated 350° oven just until eggs are firm, about 20 minutes. Serves 3 or 4 persons.

*   *   *

Who but the Spanish would think of making such a pretty dish of eggs, just to serve as a first course? It's a conceit, but rather fun.

HUEVOS ARRIBA (Puffed Eggs)

4 eggs, separated	¼ cup chopped, pimiento-
4 slices buttered toast	stuffed olives
¼ cup grated mild cheese,	¼ teaspoon salt
such as Gruyère	⅛ teaspoon pepper

Beat egg whites until stiff; add cheese, chopped olives, salt and pepper, folding in until well blended. Spoon egg whites on toast, forming a nest on each slice. Carefully slip an uncooked egg yolk in each nest. Place toast on baking sheet and bake at 325° for 20 minutes until yolk is glazed over and meringue lightly browned. An unusual dish for lunch. Must be prepared at last minute, served immediately. Serves 4 persons.

TOMATES RELLENOS AL HORNO
(Baked Stuffed Tomatoes)

6 medium tomatoes	Salt, pepper
3 tablespoons olive oil	6 eggs
Fresh or dried tarragon	

Slice the blossom end from each tomato and scoop out a little of the pulp of each. Brush all over with olive oil. Sprinkle with salt and pepper and a little minced fresh or crumbled dried tarragon. Place in oiled baking dish and bake at 375° for 20 minutes or until tomatoes are soft but still firm enough to hold their shape. Break an egg carefully into the top of each tomato. Return to oven until eggs are set but yolk still soft. Serve at once as a luncheon dish or as the first course to a dinner with roast meat as the entree. (If the latter, serve only potatoes with the roast, follow with green salad.) Serves 6.

* * *

Despite the assertion that Basque cookery is "not Spanish," as my *Madrileño* friend remarked, there is decided resemblance between this traditional Basque dish and the Spanish way of scrambling eggs with bits of meat, seafood, or vegetables mixed in.

PIPERADE (Eggs Basque Style)

½ green pepper, cut in thin strips
3 tablespoons olive oil
¼ teaspoon salt
1 small white onion, minced
1 small garlic clove, crushed
1 or 2 garden-ripe tomatoes, peeled and chopped, or 2 tablespoons tomato catsup
2 tablespoons minced ham
4 eggs, beaten until light

Sauté the pepper in olive oil over moderate heat; sprinkle with salt as it cooks. Add onion and garlic, cook until soft; add tomatoes, cook until consistency of mush (use tomato catsup when local tomatoes are not in season, adding with the ham). Add ham, cook about 20 minutes longer over very low heat. Add eggs, stirring quickly and deftly to blend with vegetables. Lift up with spatula as the egg thickens, and as soon as mixture is firm throughout, slide out onto heated plates. Makes 2 to 4 servings. Double to serve 6 persons.

CHAPTER 5

Pescados y Mariscos

(FISH AND SHELLFISH)

So wonderful is the seafood of Spain a mere chapter on the subject hardly does it justice. Never have I tasted such exquisite seafood. Day after day we ordered it in preference to meat dishes, often having a first course of *mariscos* (shellfish) and a main course of *pescados* (fish), or vice versa. Not only do they have enormous variety, but most important of all, the seafood is fresh. I was asked in Spain why Americans eat so little fish, and I had a quick answer. It is because few Americans know what really fresh fish tastes like. We are proud in the United States of our elaborate distribution system and the great variety of foods always available, but in the process we have lost the precious quality of fresh flavor. Refrigeration prevents spoilage, but inevitably flavor fades away, like the pretty, waxlike flowers in the florist cases which, when held below the nostrils, have little more scent than their artificial counter-parts.

Freezing of seafood has brought products to the hinterlands never before available, but even in our coastal areas, near oceans and lakes and streams, frozen fish and shellfish have replaced the fresh items in great measure. Frozen fish is pref-erable to fish five or six days old (as is much of the "fresh" fish in our markets), but freezing changes the texture and destroys much of the flavor. I used shrimp a great deal before going to Spain. Since returning, I have shopped everywhere trying to get shrimp which can approximate in flavor the *langostinos* and *gambas* of Spain. Alas, even the "fresh" shrimp are usually defrosted frozen shrimp, for all our shrimp now are frozen as soon as they are caught.

Going to the very best, most expensive American markets, I will ask, "When was this fish caught?" Sometimes the answer is quick, "Just came in this morning." Again a more shame-faced reply will be, "We got it in yesterday, I think." "But when was it caught?" I insist—futilely, I know. The reply can only be a shrug. How can the men in the market know? They take what they get. The American public does not insist on really fresh fish—as do the Spanish. Therefore, as long as it is not actually spoiled, fish is offered for sale, at the same price, to whoever comes shopping.

With each passing day after it is caught, fish not only loses its sweet flavor, but takes on gradually a strong, unpleasant odor. Consequently, cooks preparing the fish purchased in our markets dislike the chore. Frozen fish at least does not smell.

Let me try to explain about the different kinds of Spanish shellfish. When you see them in the markets, you recognize that a *langostino* is an entirely different crustacean from a *gamba* or a *Cegalas*. The shells are different, the claws are

different. A gamba is not simply a smaller version of a langostino. (And the Spanish langostino is completely different
from the shellfish of this name from Argentina often sold in
our markets.) There are also clams of all sizes, the sweetest
of all the tiny *almejas*. These are quite different in flavor from
our cherrystones. Lobster is called *langosta,* and compares
favorably with our Maine lobsters—though, here, I would say,
we have the advantage. I found the Spanish langosta tougher
than Maine lobster. The langosta is comparable in flavor and
texture to the South African and New Zealand rock-lobster
tail, now available throughout the U.S.

The fish of Spain also differ considerably from those found
in our markets. *Mero* is wonderfully sweet and tender. This, I
am told, is a species of perch, but nothing at all like the perch
in our markets. *Rape* (pronounced ra'-pay) has no equivalent.
It is an ugly fish, with a huge head (it is sometimes called
"frog fish"), but what delicious flesh! *Merluza,* which one
finds on every restaurant menu, is like hake, something like
fresh cod. *Lenguado* is sole, lovely, tender sole, always delicious no matter how it is prepared. *Rodaballo* is turbot, not
encountered so often as the other fish, but always sweet and
good. *Pez espada* is swordfish—exactly like that in our markets.

There are also fresh brook trout and salmon caught in cold-
water streams, and *salmonetes,* little red mullets, and fresh
sardines, and other fish too numerous to mention. I have suggested substitutes for many of these, and I have tried to make
them taste as delicious as possible, using seasonings that I
hope will mask the lack of natural fresh flavor. Alas, we can
only do with what we have. I doubt whether I will really
enjoy fish until I return to Spain again—I've been spoiled!

LANGOSTINOS AL JEREZ (Large Shrimp in Sherry Sauce)

1½ pounds large raw shrimp, already shelled and deveined
¼ cup olive oil
1 medium onion, chopped
2 tablespoons minced parsley
1 small can (4 ounces) pimientos, drained, diced fine
¾ teaspoon salt
1 garlic clove, crushed
Pinch of saffron
½ cup very dry Spanish sherry
½ cup water
1 tablespoon soft bread crumbs, very fine
¼ teaspoon powdered cumin

Fry shrimp in hot olive oil just until bright orange. Remove. Lower heat, add onion, parsley, pimiento, garlic, and salt to oil, cook until onion is soft. Let leaf saffron stand in sherry, strain. Add sherry, water, bread crumbs, and cumin to onion mixture, simmer 5 minutes until bread has thickened sauce. Return shrimp to pan, cook 2 minutes longer. Serves 4 persons.

LANGOSTINOS A LA MARINA (Large Shrimp Seashore Style)

1½ pounds raw shrimp, shelled and deveined
2 medium onions, chopped
1 green pepper, diced
2 or 3 garlic cloves, crushed
3 tablespoons olive oil
1 medium can (1 pound) peeled whole tomatoes
Salt and pepper
2 tablespoons minced parsley

Cook onions, pepper, and garlic in olive oil, over moderate heat, until tender. Add tomatoes and salt and pepper to taste. Simmer 20 minutes longer. Add shrimp, cook over *low* heat until just pink. (Do not let sauce come to a boil.) Serve with rice. Serves 4 persons.

The following exquisite way of serving langostino is a specialty of Club 31 in Madrid, a chic, very new, very modern restaurant where the service is so perfect one is made to feel like royalty.

LANGOSTINOS AL CHAMPAN
(Large Shrimp in Champagne Sauce)

20 *large raw shrimp in the shell*   4 *egg yolks*
   or 4 or 5 rock lobster tails   1 *teaspoon cornstarch*
½ *bottle champagne, or very*   4 *tablespoons butter*
   dry white wine   1 *cup light cream*
½ *teaspoon salt*   1 *teaspoon paprika*
Pinch of cayenne

Cover the shrimp or lobster tails with the champagne or
wine, add salt and cayenne. Poach gently just until shrimp are
pink. Let cool in wine. Remove from wine, saving the stock.
Discard shells of shrimp or lobster. Meantime, boil wine stock
to reduce to 1 cup. Beat egg yolks until thick, blend in cornstarch, add a little of the hot stock, then combine yolks with
remaining stock, butter, cream, and paprika. Cook slowly, stirring with a whisk, until sauce is slightly thickened and smooth.
Taste to see if additional salt is needed. Arrange the shrimp
or sliced lobster in a large shallow casserole or 4 individual
ramekins, cover with the sauce, place under broiler, 6 inches
from heat, until top is glazed and golden. Makes 4 servings.

LENGUADOS AL CHAMPAN (Sole in Champagne Sauce)

Follow the above recipe but use sole (*lenguado*) instead of
shellfish. Cut 1 pound fillet of sole in 20 strips. Poach in the
champagne or wine, exactly as above, for no more than 6 minutes, keeping heat so low that wine only "smiles," to prevent
fish from disintegrating. Let cool in the broth before attempt-
ing to remove, then use a slotted spoon, taking care that fish
does not break. Place at once in ramekins, before preparing
sauce.

CEGALAS EN GELATINA (Shrimp in Aspic)

1 pound medium raw shrimp in shells

2 cups water or vegetable stock

1 cup very dry sherry

1 small onion, peeled

½ teaspoon salt

Sprig of parsley

1 carrot, cooked

12 asparagus spears, cooked

2 envelopes unflavored gelatin

¾ cup mayonnaise

Sliced olives

Combine water or vegetable stock with ½ cup sherry, onion, and salt; bring to a boil. Add shrimp in their shells, return to boil, cook just 4 minutes, or until shells are bright pink. Cool. Remove shrimp, strain stock through cheesecloth or very fine sieve. Measure liquid; add remaining sherry to make 2½ cups altogether. Soften gelatin in 2 tablespoons cold water; dissolve in hot stock. Arrange a layer of shrimp in 1-quart ring mold. Pour enough gelatin mixture to cover; chill until firm. Mix remaining gelatin mixture with mayonnaise, beating with rotary beater until smooth. Arrange chopped asparagus spears and pieces of carrot over shrimp; cover with layer of mayonnaise mixture, chill until firm. Add more shrimp, then more mayonnaise mixture, until mold is filled to brim. Chill until firm, at least 2 hours. Unmold on lettuce. Handsome enough for a centerpiece for a luncheon party of 4. Makes 6 to 8 servings.

LANGOSTA PERPIGNAN (Lobster Perpignan Style)

2 small live lobsters, about 1 pound each, or 4 7-ounce rock lobster tails

1 chicken bouillon cube or 1 teaspoon powdered concentrate

2 tablespoons butter or olive oil

1 whole clove

4 to 6 small white onions, peeled

2 cloves garlic, minced

1 tablespoon flour

1 cup water

1 teaspoon minced parsley

Pinch of fennel or anise

Pinch of saffron

2 tablespoons tomato purée or catsup

1 teaspoon salt

½ cup very dry Spanish sherry

Add lobster to rapidly boiling salted water. If live lobsters, boil 20 minutes; if frozen lobster tails, only 5 minutes after water again comes to boil. Drain, carefully remove meat from shells. Meantime, add bouillon cube or powdered concentrate to butter, stir to dissolve, add onions, cook until glazed. Stick the whole clove in one of the onions. Add the garlic, cook a few seconds, then blend the flour into the butter, slowly add water, then the parsley, seasonings, tomato purée, and sherry. Gently simmer sauce 1 hour, reducing to half. Add sliced lobster meat just before serving, simmer until just heated through. If preferred, return meat to shells, cover with sauce. Makes 4 servings, enough for 2 persons who love lobster.

* * *

The following recipe I obtained from Angela de Domecq, whose husband is director of the Pedro Domecq bodegas in Jerez. With it was served a very, very dry sherry such as one finds only in Spain. However, Domecq's La Ina cocktail sherry will go quite as well with this lovely dish.

RAPSODIA DE MARISCOS (Rhapsody of Shellfish)

2 cans (4 ounces each) large shrimp
1 pound fillet of sole
6 tablespoons butter
½ pound small mushroom caps
3 tablespoons minced onion
1 ripe tomato, peeled and chopped
2 tablespoons flour
1 pint light cream
¼ teaspoon salt
½ cup grated mild cheese
¼ cup fine crumbs, moistened with oil or butter

Cut fish in 2 inch squares, sauté gently in 3 tablespoons of the butter until delicately golden, remove to casserole. Sauté mushrooms and onion, adding remaining butter; when onion is tender, add tomato, cook 2 minutes, stir in flour, then slowly add cream, cook until smooth. Add shrimp to the cream; add the salt, seasoning. Stir in cheese, cook until well blended. Taste for seasoning. Add to the fish in casserole. Top with oil-moistened crumbs. Place in oven 20 minutes before dinner is to be served, turn on oven to 350°, bake until crumbs are golden. Makes 4 to 6 servings.

* * *

The zarzuela is "musical comedy" in Spain (or vaudeville with musical numbers). Zarzuela de Mariscos in Barcelona is a lovely mixture of shellfish in a superb sauce, cooked to your order, brought sizzling to the table. We enjoyed it at the Restaurant Soley in the heart of downtown Barcelona, sitting at tables in a glassed-in terrace which overlooked the street. The restaurant was filled mostly with businessmen who looked as if they lived very well, indeed, ordering their wines with great seriousness, downing their oysters thoughtfully, examining the entrees brought to them as critically as art critics at a museum. Oysters here were served beautifully in baskets, with wedges of lemon inserted between the shells in an artful arrangement. Chickens turned on a spit within sight of the diners. The aromas were devastating. By the time a dish of zarzuela was placed before me, I was ravenous.

ZARZUELA DE MARISCOS (Catalonian Seafood Casserole)

1 *pound halibut or sole fillets, cut in chunks*

1 *pound already shelled raw shrimp*

1 *quart mussels in shell, or 1 can (10½ ounces) minced clams and liquid*

3 to 4 *tablespoons olive oil*

1 *tablespoon salted flour*

2 *tablespoons brandy*

1 *medium onion, chopped*

1 *pimiento, diced*

2 *garlic cloves, crushed*

3 *tablespoons blanched almonds, crushed*

2 *tomatoes, peeled and chopped, or 1 cup canned tomatoes*

1 *teaspoon salt*

½ *cup white wine*

1 *tablespoon minced parsley*

Heat 3 tablespoons olive oil in heavy pan, add fish, which has been dusted in flour, cook until lightly browned on one side, turn to brown on the other side, and add shrimp, cooking until shrimp are pink. Add brandy, set aflame, let flame die out. Remove shrimp and fish. To oil in pan add onion, pimiento, garlic, and crushed almonds, sauté until vegetables are tender, adding more oil if necessary. Add tomatoes, sprinkling with salt. Add wine, then the mussels, which have been well scrubbed and beards removed, or the clams. Bring to a boil, cook over high heat, reducing liquid to thicken the sauce, or until mussel shells open. Taste for seasoning; replace fish and shrimp in sauce, cook 2 minutes longer. Serve in large shallow casserole. Makes 6 to 8 servings, enough for 4 or 5 persons.

When I was in the Basque country in north Spain, asking to be served typical Basque dishes, I found *merluza Koskera* set before me three days in a row. The Basques consider this one of their finest offerings.

MERLUZA KOSKERA (Fish Steaks Basque Style)

2 *pounds hake, cut in steaks*	2 *cups fish stock*
½ *cup olive oil*	1 *tablespoon minced parsley*
Few drops lemon juice	1 *cup cooked peas*
2 *tablespoons flour*	8 *canned white asparagus*
1 *teaspoon salt*	*spears*
1 *or 2 garlic cloves*	4 *hard-cooked eggs*
	Lemon

Make a fish stock first of the head, tail, and bones of fish, flavoring with onion and herbs. Boil 20 minutes; drain and strain, add 2 tablespoons butter to hot stock. Marinate the hake steaks in the olive oil, sprinkling with a little lemon juice. After an hour, remove from marinade, dust with the flour blended with salt. Add some of olive oil to a casserole or skillet, sauté floured cod until lightly browned on each side. Place a peeled whole garlic clove in the skillet at the same time, until well-browned. Add a little additional oil from the marinade, if needed. Remove and discard garlic when brown. Thicken oil in casserole with remaining flour, slowly add fish stock. Add parsley. Cook gently, covered, over very low heat until fish will flake, or place in 350° oven for ½ hour. During last 10 minutes, add asparagus, peas, and quarters of hard-cooked eggs, arranging these around the cod. Serve lemon wedges on the side. Makes 6 servings or enough for 4 persons.

* * *

The following manner of preparing cod, with sherry and almonds, is Andalusian. I have even done this to frozen cod and turned that tasteless excuse for fish into something quite acceptable. The dish is even better, when you use sole or halibut.

MERLUZA AL JEREZ (Fish Steak in Sherry Sauce)

2 *pounds fresh cod, steaks or fillets (or 2 pounds fillet of sole or halibut)*
3 *tablespoons olive oil*
1 *teaspoon salt*

½ *cup medium dry sherry*
2 *tablespoons fine dry crumbs*
2 *tablespoons chopped blanched almonds*

Arrange fish in baking dish or shallow casserole that has been brushed with part of the oil. Sprinkle with salt, brush remaining oil over top of fish. (If using frozen fish, cut into serving pieces while frozen, marinate with olive oil while defrosting.) Blend together crumbs and nuts, arrange over top of fish. Place in 350° oven, bake 25 minutes or until fish flakes. Baste with sherry occasionally as it bakes. Makes 6 servings.

* * *

Seville is storybook Spain: high wrought-iron gates set in white walls, allowing a glimpse of cobblestoned courtyards and stately old-fashioned villas as you walk past, parks full of orange trees on which huge golden oranges hang all year until they drop unhindered to the ground (these are the bitter oranges of Seville, good only for marmalade or a sauce for duck or to use in making curaçao and vermouth). Palm trees line the streets, and every now and then one comes to a lovely park in the Moorish style where one may sit on mosaic-tiled benches under heavy shade, lulled into laziness by the heady perfume of geraniums and mimosa.

As charmingly unreal as an opera setting is the old Santa Cruz quarter in the heart of the city. I wandered through these narrow, twisting streets quite by chance, enchanted by the way tree branches were trained as a trellis over a pedestrian walk, by the sudden appearance of tiny be-flowered squares, by the wrought-iron balconies which almost met between buildings overhead (so narrow was the walk), nearly every balcony filled with potted geraniums.

The streets wound like a labyrinth until I was quite lost and wondered whether I should ever find my way out, then suddenly I was walking through a high archway into the plaza before the cathedral. Later I learned this had once been Seville's Jewish quarter. It adjoins the alcazar, and the reason for this, I was told, was that when Peter the Cruel was King of Spain he chose as his secretary a Jew, and the secretary naturally had to live within easy access of the palace—the alcazar built earlier by the Moors, taken over by Peter for his use.

Seville is a city romantic in a decadent way, slumbering, easygoing, its walls beginning to crumble here and there, its people slow to act. Yet many of the restaurants are strikingly modern in décor, sparkling new. Such is the influence of tourism: romantic Seville is a tourist attraction, and tourists are always interested in good food.

The Coliseo Restaurant, for example, located within easy walking distance of the Santa Cruz quarter, has a window wall two stories high, rising over a busy street. As in virtually every restaurant in Seville, the street-level floor is given over to the bar, a long bar, and to what is called in Spain a *cafetería* (though not what we mean by cafeteria at all), where quick-lunch service is available at small vinyl-topped tables. Then one walks up a circular, open staircase to the dining room, where tables are set with white cloths and waiters render quiet, efficient service.

I dined that day on what was called on the menu "*Tronco de Merluza Tropical.*" It turned out to be a most elaborate dish, steaks of fish served up with a mélange of bananas and raisins, pineapple and almonds—much more Caribbean than Spanish. Later, while in this area, I noted many Latin-American influences in the food, the use of coconut, for example, and of rum and curaçao as flavorings. I was told there is more feeling of kinship with Latin America in this part of Spain than anywhere else, partly because ships going to and from South America dock at the nearby ports of Cádiz and Algeciras, but also perhaps because it was from Cádiz that the navigators and conquistadores set sail for the west, back in the fifteenth and sixteenth centuries, Spain's period of glory. Seville was Spain's capital in those days. The décor which we considered typically "Spanish," the filigree work and lacy mantillas and heavy embroidery, came from Seville at a time when the Spanish influence was strongest in the New World. The foods of the New World were apparently absorbed into the cuisine of Andalusia just as readily during that time when Spain was so proud of its overseas empire. The restaurant in which I sat was as utterly modern in décor as a place could be, yet its food suggested sailing ships and dashing caballeros and an era of romance that Andalusia has never lost.

TRONCO DE MERLUZA TROPICAL (Fish Steaks Tropical)

1½ pounds halibut steak or haddock
Lemon
1 tablespoon butter
3 tablespoons olive oil
8 small bananas
16 blanched almonds, chopped
1 teaspoon grated onion
¼ cup muscatel seeded raisins
1 teaspoon minced parsley
1 small can pineapple chunks, drained
¼ cup water
¼ cup very dry sherry
Salt to taste

Cut fish into serving pieces, sprinkle with salt, and sauté gently in the olive oil and butter until delicately colored. Transfer to shallow casserole, sprinkling with a few drops of lemon juice. Slice bananas lengthwise, sauté in the oil and butter until lightly browned, place around fish. Add nuts and onion to pan, cook 1 minute, add remaining ingredients, boil up, scraping all bits from bottom; taste for seasoning. Pour over fish in casserole. Place in 325° oven for 15 minutes. Serves 4.

FILETE DE LENGUADO RELLENO (Stuffed Fillet of Sole)

SAUCE

6 fillets of sole
1 cup soft bread crumbs
1 rock lobster tail, cooked, minced
2 tablespoons olive oil
¼ teaspoon salt
¼ cup minced parsley
1 tablespoon onion
Pinch of orégano
6 almonds, chopped
¼ cup chopped onion
2 tablespoons olive oil
1 garlic clove
1 tablespoon minced parsley
1 8-ounce can (1 cup) tomato sauce
1 tablespoon medium dry sherry
½ teaspoon powdered beef bouillon concentrate or ½ bouillon cube

Combine the bread, minced lobster, olive oil, salt, parsley, 1 tablespoon onion, orégano, and almonds. Place 1 to 1½ tablespoons of this mixture on each fillet of sole, roll up, starting with the narrow end, and place in individual squares of foil (12 by 12 inches) with overlapped side of fillet on the bottom. For the sauce, meantime, cook onion in 2 tablespoons olive oil until tender; place the peeled whole garlic clove in the oil at the same time, but remove the garlic when brown and discard. Add remaining ingredients to sauce, cook until reduced one-third. Spoon 2 tablespoons of the sauce over each stuffed fillet, crimp edges of foil to seal. Bake in preheated 350° oven 25 to 30 minutes. Makes 6 servings.

* * *

The following recipe was given me by Señora José Ybarra of Seville as a family specialty. It is a strange yet delicious combination of ingredients.

LENGUADO YBARRA (Fillet of Sole Ybarra)

1½ pounds flounder or sole
    fillets
1 pound spinach
Pinch of nutmeg
⅛ teaspoon salt
1 tablespoon cream

4 large bananas
¼ cup olive oil
8 canned white asparagus tips
¾ teaspoon salt
béchamel sauce (see Index)

Thoroughly wash and drain spinach; sprinkle with nutmeg and ⅛ teaspoon salt, cook covered just until limp. Drain, chop fine. Blend with cream, purée in electric blender or force through sieve or food mill. Arrange puréed spinach over bottom of large round shallow casserole. Slice bananas lengthwise, then cut each slice in half crosswise. Sauté in the olive oil until lightly browned. Place at either end of the casserole, over the spinach. Sauté the flounder or sole (previously cut into long strips) in the oil, sprinkling with ¾ teaspoon salt; lift carefully and place over the spinach. Arrange the asparagus spears between strips of fish. Place casserole in warm (275°) oven while preparing béchamel sauce. Pour sauce over fish, spinach, etc. Place 4 inches from heat under broiler until lightly glazed and serve at once. Makes 6 servings.

Note: As a short cut, 2 packages of frozen creamed spinach may be used in place of fresh spinach puréed and creamed.

PESCADO RELLENO AL TOREADOR
(Bullfighter's Stuffed Fish)

1 whole fish, dressed, 4 to 5
    pounds (bass, pompano, or
    bluefish)
1 cup olive oil
1 clove garlic, minced
1 onion, chopped fine
1 can shrimp, drained, minced
½ cup minced ham
1 cup stale bread crumbs

¼ teaspoon salt
¼ cup minced parsley
⅛ teaspoon black pepper
¼ teaspoon thyme
¼ teaspoon nutmeg
Juice ½ lemon
½ green pepper, sliced
6 to 8 medium shrimp, shelled,
    cooked, deveined

Heat ½ cup of the olive oil in heavy skillet, add to it garlic, onion, shrimp, and ham, sauté until onion is soft, using moderate heat. Add bread crumbs, salt, parsley, black pepper, thyme, and nutmeg. Cook, stirring, until crumbs are golden. Stuff the fish loosely with the mixture, sew up with thread or truss with small skewers and twine. Pour remaining oil in a baking pan and place fish in the pan. Add lemon juice and green pepper. Bake at 350° for 40 minutes; fish should be firm to touch. Baste frequently as it cooks with olive oil in bottom of pan to brown the skin. Place whole cooked shrimp over top of fish on platter as garnish, sprinkle fish with minced parsley, arrange lemon wedges around edge. Makes 8 servings (ample for 4).

LOBINA EN PAPEL (Bass Baked in Foil)

1 whole sea bass, dressed, 4 to
   5 pounds
½ cup olive oil
1 cup soft bread crumbs
2 tablespoons minced parsley

1 medium onion, minced
¼ cup sliced mushrooms
6 stuffed green olives, sliced
1 tablespoon capers
Salt and pepper

Have fish man split fish open to remove center bone. Brush inside with half the olive oil, sprinkle fish with salt from shaker and with freshly ground pepper. Combine remaining olive oil with remaining ingredients, blending well. Spread out dressing in center of very large piece of heavy-duty aluminum foil, place fish in center so that it will be covered top and bottom with the dressing when foil is sealed. Fold over foil, crimp edges to seal securely. Bake at 400° for 30 minutes. Open foil: fish should be firm to touch when baked. Will serve 3 or 4 persons.

* * *

Mero is a marvelously sweet, juicy fish listed frequently on restaurant menus in north Spain. Our halibut is similar enough to it that it can be used as a substitute. I have prepared each of the three following recipes a number of times in my home, and like them better each time.

MERO A LA MONTANA (Fish, Mountain Style)

4 halibut steaks
1 dozen medium-sized raw
   shrimp, shelled and deveined
3 tablespoons olive oil
2 small white onions, minced
1 tablespoon minced parsley

¼ teaspoon thyme
⅛ teaspoon rosemary
⅛ teaspoon basil
1 teaspoon salt
½ cup white wine

Simmer onions in olive oil until soft but not brown. Add herbs, salt, and wine, simmer 10 minutes. Strain, pour into shallow casserole or baking dish. Place halibut steaks in strained sauce, sprinkle top with additional olive oil, place uncooked shrimp over top of fish, three shrimp on each steak. Cover dish with foil, place in 300° oven, bake 20 to 25 minutes. Remove foil, bake 5 minutes longer. Shrimp should be bright pink. Sprinkle with a little minced parsley, serve with lemon wedges. 4 servings.

MERO A LA PASTELERA (Fish, Baker Style)

3 pounds halibut (tail end)	½ garlic clove, minced
1 lemon, sliced	¼ cup chopped blanched
⅓ cup Spanish olive oil	almonds
Salt	1 tablespoon minced onion
1 tablespoon minced parsley	½ teaspoon paprika
1 slice white bread, crumbled	¼ teaspoon salt
fine	½ cup tomato sauce

Cut incisions in top of fish, insert the lemon slices. Sprinkle fish all over with salt. Brush bottom of long shallow casserole with half of the olive oil, lay fish in casserole and brush top of fish with some of oil from bottom of dish. Cover fish with mixture of parsley, crumbs, garlic, almonds, onion, paprika, ¼ teaspoon salt, and remaining oil, pressing dressing down into skin. Bake at 350° for 15 minutes; add tomato sauce, bake 30 minutes longer or until fish is firm when touched. Baste once or twice during baking. Makes 6 to 8 servings.

PESCADO FRITO (Fried Fillet)

6 fillets of halibut, sole, or red	2 tablespoons water
snapper	½ teaspoon salt
4 tablespoons flour	Olive oil
2 eggs, separated	

Trim fillets and cut into serving-size pieces. Blend flour, egg yolks, and salt, beat until smooth, stirring in water. Separately beat egg whites until stiff. Fold egg whites into yolk mixture. Dip each fillet into this foamy batter then fry in olive oil ½ inch deep in heavy skillet until golden on each side. 6 delicious servings.

PEZ ESPADA (Swordfish)

1 pound swordfish, thinly sliced	1 tablespoon minced parsley
	1 garlic clove, crushed
1 cup Spanish olive oil	½ teaspoon salt
2 tablespoons lemon juice	1 tablespoon finely chopped
2 tablespoons vinegar	onion

Place swordfish in deep bowl, cover with remaining ingredients, marinate several hours. Remove from marinade, arrange on foil, place 4 inches from heat in preheated broiler oven (with reduced flame) and brown lightly on each side, cooking 5 to 7 minutes altogether. Pass marinade as a sauce. Makes 2 to 4 servings. Delicious!

* * *

Philip V was the first Bourbon king of Spain, grandson of Louis XIV of France. He brought to Spain with him the grandeur of the French court and the French preoccupation with fine food—though he and his heirs were never happily accepted by the people of Spain. This manner of cooking trout, named for the Bourbon ruler, is a specialty at the Mesón de Cándido restaurant in Segovia.

TRUCHAS FELIPE V (Trout in the Style of Philip V)

Dust six small trout with flour which has been blended with a little salt. Cut 3 slices bacon in half (or cut 6 slivers of lean ham). Add oil to a heavy skillet to a depth of ½ inch— preferably olive oil. Heat until a crust of bread will brown in 1½ minutes. Add bacon, cook until crisp, remove, and drain (cook ham slivers until delicately browned). Add the trout to the hot oil, cook quickly, turning to brown evenly. Place on paper to drain, inserting the ham or bacon in the cavity of each. While the fish is cooking, place parsley sprigs in ice water. Remove from the water, pat dry with paper towel. Drop parsley in hot oil. It will be crisp in seconds. Drain on absorbent paper. Serve as garnish for the fish, along with lemon wedges. For 6 persons.

* * *

There are more hunting and fishing preserves in Spain than in any other country of Europe, which accounts for such items as trout, salmon, partridge, and other small birds appearing frequently on restaurant menus. Smoked salmon is sometimes offered as an *entremeses;* so is pickled salmon. This is river salmon, not as large as our Pacific salmon, but equally delicious. For us in America, the salmon steaks available in fish markets can be used, with magnificent results. This is a favorite recipe of mine—delicious when baked in the oven, even better when cooked over charcoal out of doors.

SALMON AL HORNO (Salmon Baked in Sauce)

6 *salmon steaks, ¾ inch thick*	1 *teaspoon salt*
½ *cup medium dry sherry*	A *few shreds anise or fennel*
½ *cup olive oil*	⅛ *teaspoon thyme*
1 *tablespoon vinegar*	1 *tablespoon minced parsley*

Combine all ingredients, place salmon steaks each in a 10-inch square of foil, spoon one-sixth of the marinade mixture over each. Crimp foil to seal, let salmon marinate in the mixture for several hours, all day if possible. Bake in preheated 375° oven for 25 minutes; or in summer, out of doors, if a double thickness of foil is used it can be placed just above the glowing coals of a charcoal fire. Serve the salmon in its sauce to 6 persons.

Note: Equally delicious are the salmon steaks grilled over charcoal after long marinating in the sauce, cooked just until golden on each side, the fish flaking easily.

* * *

Bacalao—salt cod—is used extensively in Spain. I have discovered it can be purchased here in Italian and Spanish markets, but there are two different kinds (perhaps more!). Certain types require longer soaking than others; some have bones, some have been filleted before drying. A liking for bacalao is, I suspect, an acquired taste, for even when I ordered it in Spain, I could not become wildly enthusiastic about it. To me it seemed too salty, too tough. However, those who like it grow quite lyrical in its praise.

I have tried using frozen cod in place of bacalao, with variable results. Once or twice the dish has been so bad (made with frozen cod) I have had to throw it out altogether. Again, it has turned out to be delicious. Perhaps the frozen product itself is to be blamed. Anyway, I cannot recommend the substitution. For those who like bacalao, here are recipes I can recommend. The sauce in each case is excellent!

Most famous of all is *bacalao vizcaína,* named for the province of Viscaya in the Basque country.

BACALAO A LA VIZCAINA (Salt Cod, Vizcaya Style)

1 *pound dried salt cod*
¾ *to 1 cup olive oil*
2 *cloves garlic*
2 *slices bread, cubed*
6 *pimientos*

1 *large or 2 medium onions, sliced*
1 *large can (1 pound 12 ounces) peeled, whole tomatoes, best quality*
½ *cup stock*

Beat dried cod by hitting it against a counter for a dozen whacks (this breaks the tissue, making the fish softer when cooked). Soak the cod in water overnight; drain, add clear cold water, bring slowly to the boil (over moderate heat), then lower heat, keeping water at a gentle simmer, just "smiling," for 15 to 20 minutes. Drain, reserving ½ cup of this stock. If there are bones in the cod, carefully remove them, then place fish in the heated olive oil and cook until golden. Remove carefully, drain on paper towel. Cook onion, garlic, bread cubes, and pimiento in the same oil until onion is tender. Add the drained whole tomatoes, chopped, cook about 20 minutes over low heat. Add reserved tomato juice and stock as sauce thickens. Place sauce and codfish in layers in casserole. Scatter bread crumbs which have been sautéed in olive oil over top. Bake in preheated 325° oven for 20 to 25 minutes. Makes 4 servings.

BACALAO DE ALCANTARA (Codfish Alcántara Style)

1 pound dried salt codfish	¼ teaspoon salt or to taste
3 tablespoons flour	2 tablespoons minced parsley
½ cup olive oil	12 sliced, pimiento-stuffed
2 large potatoes, thickly sliced	olives
2 medium onions, thinly sliced	1 cup water
	1 hard-cooked egg, sliced

Beat cod by whacking against counter top to soften. Soak in water 12 to 24 hours; drain, cover with cold fresh water, bring just to a boil, turn off heat, let stand in hot water 15 minutes; drain. (Remove any bones in cod at this stage.) Dust cod with flour, fry in olive oil until golden; remove. Fry potatoes and onions in same oil, sprinkling with salt. When vegetables are tender, replace fried cod, top with parsley and olives, add 1 cup water. Simmer gently, without allowing to boil, shaking pan frequently, until sauce is thickened. Serve garnished with slices of hard-cooked egg. Makes 3 or 4 servings.

Seafood Sauces

Really fresh seafood is good no matter how it is prepared, and often the best way to enjoy it is to cook it simply, then serve it with a sauce or a choice of several sauces.

A survey made by the U. S. Fish and Wildlife Service a few years ago revealed that 75 per cent of American families cook fish just one way: they fry it. Usually this means breading the fish first, or at least dusting it with flour.

For those concerned with calories, or with heartburn, or other dietary problems, it is well to remember there are half a dozen other, equally simple ways of cooking fish. There is poaching—an art virtually unknown to Americans. This means cooking the fish gently (never allowing the liquid to boil) in fish stock or a combination of water, wine, and herbs. It may be done in the oven or on the top of stove, whichever is most convenient. Especially to be recommended for white-fleshed, delicately flavored fish such as sole, halibut, turbot, or even really fresh cod.

There are also baking and broiling. Broiling tends to dry out fish, so it needs to be marinated first, then basted with butter, oil, or the marinating mixture as it cooks. Baked fish is the easiest of all. Simply brush it well with oil, dust with salt and pepper, and slip in the oven, bake until the skin is firm to the touch (if fish is whole) or flesh flakes easily with a fork.

All seafood is low in calories. The "gourmet" shellfish, lobster, shrimp, and crab, have become very expensive, but most fish still remains moderate in price. Good for those conscious of both waistlines and pocketbooks to keep in mind.

SALSA HERNANDEZ (Sauce Hernandez)

1 hard-cooked egg yolk	1 teaspoon prepared mustard
1 raw egg yolk	2 tablespoons olive oil
½ teaspoon salt	½ tablespoon vinegar

Mash cooked egg yolk, blend with raw egg yolk, then slowly beat in salt, mustard, and olive oil. Finally add vinegar. A bit like mayonnaise in flavor but quicker and easier to make, with a more distinctive egg flavor. Makes ¼ cup, enough for 4 servings.

SALSA DE TOMATE (Tomato Sauce)

4 tablespoons olive oil	2 tablespoons mixed fresh gar-
2 garlic cloves, crushed	den herbs, such as parsley,
1 medium onion, minced	basil, thyme, dill, or tarra-
1 green pepper, or 1 canned	gon
pimiento, minced	½ teaspoon salt, or to taste
6 to 8 peeled, sun-ripened	Freshly ground black pepper
tomatoes, chopped	

Sauté garlic and onion in olive oil until onion is tender; add pepper or pimiento and chopped tomatoes, herbs, salt and pepper. Simmer uncovered over low heat until sauce is thickened. Purée by beating in electric blender, if desired. Delicious both cold and hot. Makes about 1 cup.

ALI-OLI SAUCE (Garlic Sauce)

I was told in Spain that the true *ali-oli* sauce is made simply with garlic, oil, and lemon juice, no egg at all. This means, however, using a prodigious amount of garlic—and I personally find the ali-oli of Spain too potent to be edible. Even in the following version, one must be an *aficionado* of garlic. It is good, not only with seafood (try it sometime with boiled shrimp as an appetizer) and baked or poached fish, but also may be used on grilled lamb and is even good with hamburgers.

3 or 4 garlic cloves, crushed   1 tablespoon lemon juice
1 cup olive oil   ¼ teaspoon salt
1 raw egg

Force garlic cloves through press, or crush with mortar and pestle. Add ¼ cup of the olive oil, beating until smooth. Place in electric blender or in small bowl of electric mixer, with the raw egg, slowly add remaining oil while blender or mixer is in motion, until it becomes emulsified, creamy and smooth, like mayonnaise. Add lemon juice and salt after sauce has thickened. Makes ½ pint (1 cup).

SALSA DE ESPINACAS (Raw Spinach Sauce)

½ pound raw spinach   4 tablespoons olive oil
1 green pepper, diced   ¼ teaspoon salt
2 tablespoons chopped onion   1 teaspoon vinegar

Coarsely chop spinach, place in electric blender a handful at a time, with blender at low speed. Add green pepper and chopped onion, and when mixture is puréed, slowly add the olive oil and finally the salt and vinegar. This will be of relish consistency, not smooth. Makes 1½ cups.

SALSA DE ACEITE (Olive-oil Sauce)

The simplest of all sauces for fish and one of the best is a pure virgin olive oil dribbled over broiled or poached fish hot from the fire. Add a few drops of lemon juice, squeezed from a fresh-cut wedge, and a sprinkling of salt, if you like. Be sure the oil is top-grade, virgin olive oil—on this its success depends.

SALSA VERDE I (Green Sauce I)

1 cup minced parsley	1 tablespoon lemon juice or 2
1/4 cup olive oil	tablespoons vinegar
1/4 teaspoon salt	

Crush minced parsley in mortar with pestle, add olive oil a little at a time, beating until smooth. Add salt and lemon juice or vinegar. Makes 1/2 cup of a thick, pungent sauce for fried or baked, broiled or poached fish.

SALSA VERDE II (Green Sauce II)

1 small onion, minced	1/4 cup water
3 tablespoons olive oil	Pinch of saffron
1 cup minced parsley	Pinch of cayenne pepper
1/4 cup dry white wine	1/4 teaspoon salt

Cook onion in olive oil until soft without browning. Add parsley, cook until soft, about 30 seconds. Add remaining ingredients, simmer 5 minutes. Purée in electric blender until smooth (or force through food mill or sieve). Chill. Makes 3/4 cup.

SALSA AMARILLA (Yellow Sauce)

6 hard-cooked eggs	1/2 tablespoon vinegar
2 tablespoons sherry	1/4 teaspoon salt
2 tablespoons olive oil	1/2 teaspoon dry mustard
1/4 teaspoon concentrated beef bouillon powder, dissolved in 1 tablespoon hot water	

Separate cooked whites from yolks; mince whites or purée in blender. Mash yolks, add sherry, beating until smooth, then beat in oil drop by drop until creamy. Add dissolved bouillon, vinegar, salt, and mustard. Finally beat in egg whites. Makes a little less than 1/2 cup.

SALSA COLORADA (Red Sauce)

1 or 2 garlic cloves
1 pimiento, well drained
1 slice white bread, crusts removed

4 tablespoons olive oil
4 tablespoons dry white wine
Salt to taste

Mash garlic in mortar until paste-like; remove skins. Add the pimiento, mash with the garlic to a paste. Soak bread in water to cover until sponge-like, then squeeze out water and add bread to the garlic paste, mashing again. Beat in the olive oil, then thin with the wine. Purée in blender, if desired. Add salt to taste. Makes about ½ cup.

SALSA A LA GRANADINA (Sauce Granada)

1 medium tomato, peeled and chopped
1 small onion, quartered
⅛ teaspoon cumin

1 teaspoon dried mint, powdered between fingers, or 1 tablespoon minced fresh mint
Salt to taste

Place vegetables in blender, beat until puréed; add cumin, mint, and salt, beat briefly again to blend thoroughly. Makes about ⅓ cup.

SALSA ROMESCO (Sauce Romesco)

This is a specialty of the Costa Brava and frequently is freatured on menus in Barcelona restaurants. Very potent of garlic, but excellent with grilled *langostino* or lobster.

4 large tomatoes
10 blanched almonds
4 or 5 garlic cloves, crushed
2 tablespoons grated onion and juice

1 teaspoon salt, or to taste
1 jar or can (4 ounces) pimientos, well drained
1 cup olive oil
½ cup vinegar

Place whole tomatoes in oven to bake until soft. Toast almonds in the oven at the same time. When tomatoes are soft, remove, cool, put through sieve. Crush garlic cloves in mortar with toasted almonds, add the onion, salt, and the pimientos one by one. Mash to a paste with the pestle. Combine this with the sieved tomato, oil, and vinegar. Beat until smooth. Makes about 2½ cups, will keep in refrigerator for some time. Serve cold.

MAYONESA (Mayonnaise)

Mayonnaise made at home with fragrant olive oil and fresh lemon juice is an altogether different sauce from that we buy in jars at American markets. With a blender or electric mixer it is really quite easy to make and I feel well worth the trouble. Especially wonderful with lobster.

2 egg yolks	*1 teaspoon lemon juice or*
1 teaspoon prepared mustard	*vinegar*
½ teaspoon salt	*Freshly ground black pepper*
2 cups olive oil	*Pinch of cayenne pepper*

Place egg yolks, mustard, and salt in blender or small bowl of electric mixer, place in motion at low speed, add olive oil drop by drop at first (there are cruets imported from Spain, now available in housewares departments, which give out oil a drop at a time, very convenient for use in making mayonnaise). As mixture thickens, add olive oil in thin stream. When quite thick, add lemon juice or vinegar, black pepper, and cayenne pepper, continue beating until all olive oil is used. Makes 1 pint (2 cups).

Note: Many blender recipes now advise placing egg yolks, vinegar or lemon juice, and oil in the blender at the beginning and do not stress this very slow addition of oil. However, I have found that when I made mayonnaise by this method it tended to be much thinner and for some reason did not remain fresh as long. I prefer the thick mayonnaise, and the drop-by-drop method of adding the oil is not hard when the blender or mixer is doing most of the work.

BECHAMEL SAUCE

The name is French, and the sauce is essentially what we know as white sauce. Nevertheless, it is so much used in Spanish cooking it needs to be included. *Béchamel* usually appears as an ingredient in other recipes, but the sauce can be served hot over poached fish, for an entree of delicate flavor.

3 tablespoons butter	1 teaspoon salt
3 tablespoons flour	Pinch of grated nutmeg
1 cup milk	Pinch of white or black pepper
½ cup light cream	

Melt butter, stir in flour, cook over low heat until it begins to turn golden. Add the milk a little at a time, stirring until smooth after each addition; then stir in cream and seasonings. Cook about 10 minutes over very low heat, stirring occasionally. Sometimes an egg yolk is added to the sauce, after it has thickened: add a little hot sauce to the egg yolk first, then combine the 2. Makes 1½ cups sauce. (Double all ingredients when 3 cups of sauce are needed.)

CHAPTER 6

Arroz

(RICE)

Drive down the Levante or eastern coast of Spain, southward from Barcelona, and you travel first through orange groves, acres and acres of trees heavy with the sweetest and juiciest oranges of Spain, then between paddy fields where bright green sheaves of growing rice shoot up through the marshy water, and finally into an arid, red-soiled region marked by olive groves and date-palm trees. Still farther south, in the rocky, fierce mountains of Murcia, fields of crocuses produce saffron, that most expensive of all the world's spices. All these products find their way into the Levantine kitchens. The rice dishes of Spain, of which *paella* has become the most renowned, originated here.

I was surprised during my visit to Spain to observe that almost the only rice dish appearing on restaurant menus in

the Madrid region, and even in southwestern Spain, was paella. It was not until I reached Málaga in the south, whose
provincial boundaries are geographically closer to the Levante, that I found the first *arroz* section on a restaurant
menu. Potatoes are used much more than rice in most
Spanish cooking. But along the Levante coast, and especially
in the Valencia region, rice is king.

Paella is sometimes called *arroz a la valenciana*, for it was
in Valencia that this dish, combining chicken, shellfish,
meat, and vegetables in a single big iron skillet, was born,
no one knows how many centuries ago. Barcelona is also noted
for its paella, but chicken has a much less important role in
the paella of Barcelona than in that of Valencia. In fact, there
is fierce rivalry between the two cities as to whose paella is
the better—to say nothing of the rivalries among chefs and
home cooks throughout the region, for paella is rarely made
the same way twice.

The Spanish way of cooking paella is fascinating to watch.
One night we went to the Barcelona restaurant, Los Caracoles,
entering this renowned establishment through its kitchen.
Half a dozen different cooks were at the enormous black
range, red-faced from the heat of the stove, handling skillets
with a dexterity that held me spellbound. One would lift a
stove lid and place a pan directly over the fire, which was
burning at red-orange intensity, turn his attention to a second
pan, also full of sizzling food, move a third pan from its
exposed position over the fire to another spot on the cooler
part of the range. Then suddenly a flip, and an omelet was
landed neatly on a waiting plate; another swift flip, and
seafood sizzling in a skillet hopped up and back again (they
shake the pan instead of stirring to prevent food from sticking, a trick I wish I could master). Then rice was dumped
into a seafood mixture, casually, and another quick flip pre-
vented it from sticking. Water was poured on, causing a

cloud of steam to billow, then the pan was placed over a roaring hot spot on the stove.

We became too hungry to watch longer, walked inside the ancient dining room, whose walls were plastered with signed photographs of famous guests, and ordered a first course of snails, the dish for which the restaurant is named. The snails here are totally unlike the snails of French restaurants, served floating in a rich brown sauce, lusciously good. It was not much of a wait until the paella came, the *paella sin historias* (paella without history) which is a specialty at Los Cara-coles. The name apparently means that it is made impulsively, not according to any set recipe, for the dish as served to us that night was quite different from the way a friend had de-scribed his paella, enjoyed on another occasion.

Later, in Barcelona, Señor Victor O'Kelly of the Alhambra Travel Agency, a dedicated amateur chef, gave me important pointers on the proper way of cooking a paella. After you have sautéed the seafood, meat, and other ingredients that go into the dish, you add the rice, give it a quick stir, then pour in *boiling* water. The rice is cooked hard for 10 to 15 minutes (depending on the type of rice used), then put at the back of the stove, or in a warm place, for another 10 minutes. The Spanish cooks *never* cover the paella pan. It is the pan which gives the dish its name, a large, shallow iron skillet with a handle on either side. Some cooks prefer a heavy iron skillet about 2 inches deep. But always the rice is served in the same dish in which it cooked, brought to the table the instant it is ready to serve. I tried making paella this way and it worked beautifully—except that I found it better to cover the pan dur-ing the last stage, to keep the rice moist.

After dining on paella several times in Spain, I could only conclude that Americans have turned this simple dish into an unnecessarily complex operation. Essentially paella is a rice casserole to which almost anything that suits your fancy can be added (the dish known as "Spanish rice" the world over). The entire cooking time need be no more than 45 minutes. Instead of big pieces of chicken, difficult to handle, the chicken may be chopped into 2-inch chunks. Or chicken may be omitted entirely, and lean pork or veal used instead. One version of paella served in Barcelona, made without any bones, is called *parellade* (pronounced par-e-ya'-deh). For dainty eaters, this has special attraction.

Less saffron is used in the Barcelona paella—so little, in fact, that the slightly acrid flavor of saffron can scarcely be detected. Farther south, the rice is always a vivid yellow with saffron and the dish reveals more of the Moorish influence so strong throughout southern Spain.

PAELLA A LA VALENCIANA (Paella Valencia Style)

1 chicken, 2½ pounds	2 or 3 garlic cloves, crushed
½ teaspoon saffron	1 pimiento, cut in strips
1 onion	2 tomatoes, peeled and
1 tablespoon flour	chopped
½ teaspoon salt	2 cups uncooked rice
½ cup olive oil	4½ cups boiling-hot chicken
1½ pounds large raw shrimp,	broth
already shelled	1 can (7 or 8 ounces) minced
1 cup chopped ham or sliced	clams and juice
chorizo	½ package frozen peas
1 medium onion, minced	Additional salt to taste

Put aside the chicken breasts, drumsticks, upper joints, and wings of chicken. Use remaining pieces for making chicken broth, cover with 5 cups water, add 1 peeled onion, 1½ teaspoons salt, ½ teaspoon saffron; boil 30 minutes, strain, measure to make 4½ cups. Meantime, cut tender pieces of chicken in small pieces, right through the bone (or ask your butcher to do this for you when you buy the chicken). Dust chicken pieces with flour and ½ teaspoon salt; cook in olive oil in heavy skillet until crisply brown and tender. (Add a few slices of onion to oil to prevent spattering.) Remove chicken to a large casserole. Add shrimp and ham or chorizo (garlic-flavored sausage) to skillet, cook in oil until lightly browned. Remove shrimp and ham to casserole. Add onion, garlic, pimiento, and tomatoes to skillet, cook until onion is tender. Add rice, stir to glaze. Add boiling-hot chicken broth and the clams right from the can; bring again to the boil, cook 5 minutes. Add the peas, cook 5 minutes longer uncovered; transfer to casserole, rearranging some of chicken and shrimp over top of rice. Cover casserole, place over very low heat or in 300° oven 15 to 20 minutes until all liquid is absorbed. (Mussels, fresh clams, and squid are used in Spain, but mussels and squid are hard to find in our markets and our fresh clams tend to be tough when cooked this way—the canned clams are preferable.) Makes 8 to 10 servings, enough to serve 5 or 6 persons.

PAELLA A LA CATALONIA (Paella Catalan Style)

1 whole chicken breast, boned	1 or 2 garlic cloves, crushed
¼ pound lean pork	Pinch of saffron
4 tablespoons olive oil	1½ cups rice
1 small onion, minced	1 cup shelled peas or chopped
3 lobster tails	green beans
1 large tomato, peeled and	2 teaspoons salt
chopped (or 2 tablespoons	12 mussels, well scrubbed
catsup or tomato sauce)	2¾ cups boiling water

Chop both chicken breast and pork in 1-inch squares. Sauté chicken, pork, and onion in olive oil until crisply brown. Cut each lobster tail in three pieces, right through shell, cutting away undershell. Add lobster, tomato, and garlic, cook 2 minutes. Dissolve saffron in 2 tablespoons boiling water, strain, add with rice, peas, salt, and mussels, stir to coat rice with oil.

Pour on boiling water and again bring to boil, cook over moderately high heat 10 minutes. Stir or shake to prevent sticking, cover tightly, keep in a warm place on stove 15 to 20 minutes longer until all liquid is absorbed. (A very heavy skillet or cast-iron casserole will hold enough heat to complete cooking the rice; with a less heavy utensil it may be necessary to have very low heat under it during this last stage—or place skillet or casserole in an oven set at 300°.) Can be cooked entirely in a 10-inch skillet or similarly sized utensil. Makes 6 to 8 servings, enough for 4 persons.

PARELLADE (Paella Without Bones)

1 *whole chicken breast, boned, or ¼ pound diced veal*
¼ *pound chicken livers or lean ham*
¼ *pound lean pork, diced*
¼ *cup olive oil*
1 *garlic clove, minced*
1 *pimiento, drained and diced*
1 *tomato, peeled and chopped*
½ *package frozen baby Limas*
1½ *cups rice*
2¾ *cups boiling broth or water and 1½ teaspoons salt*
¼ *teaspoon saffron*
1 *can (7 or 8 ounces) minced clams and juice*
1 *can (4½ ounces) large shrimp, drained*

Cut chicken breast or veal into 1-inch pieces. Sauté with the chicken livers and pork in olive oil until lightly browned. Add garlic, pimiento, and tomato, cook about 1 minute. Add Limas, defrosted just enough to break up, and rice; stir to coat rice with oil. Add saffron to broth or water, combine with clams and juice, bring to a boil; pour boiling hot over rice. Bring liquid again to a boil, cook 10 to 15 minutes over moderately high heat, then add shrimp, cover, keep in warm place, or transfer to preheated 300° oven, leave for 10 minutes or until rice is fluffy and tender. Can be cooked in a 10-inch skillet. Enough to serve 4.

* * *

The following *arroz* is a specialty of the Costa del Sol, the southern coast of Spain, across from Africa. I dined on it one night in a well-known seafood restaurant, Playas de El Palo, a short distance form the city of Málaga, sitting on the glassed-in terrace which overlooks the sea. The moon was enormous and very yellow that night, and the white caps of waves glittered silver above the inky blackness of the sea. The boom of the surf was gentle. We had to wait half an hour for the arroz to be cooked, no hardship at all in that peaceful, lovely setting.

ARROZ CON MARISCOS Y LOMO
(Rice with Shellfish and Pork)

2 lobster tails, or ½ pound large shrimp, shelled	1 cup rice
	¼ teaspoon saffron
¼ pound lean pork, diced	1 teaspoon salt, or to taste
2 garlic cloves, peeled	2½ cups boiling water
3 or 4 tablespoons olive oil	1 can (7 ounces) minced clams
1 pimiento, diced	and juice
1 medium onion, sliced	1 tablespoon minced parsley

If lobster tails are used, cut into thirds, right through shell. Cut pork into ½-inch cubes. In heavy skillet heat oil with garlic; when garlic is browned, discard. Add pork to oil, cook until lightly browned. Add pimiento and onion, cook until onion is soft. Add lobster, cook until shell begins to turn red. Add rice, stir to coat with oil. Meantime, add saffron and salt to water, bring to a boil, add to rice with clams and juice. Bring again to a boil, cook 10 minutes over moderately high heat; add parsley, cover, reduce heat to *very* low or place in 300° oven for 15 minutes until rice is fluffy. (The Málaga dish also contained squid, which I have omitted because it is so rarely sold in our markets.) Makes 4 to 6 servings, enough for 3 or 4 persons.

ARROZ CON POLLO (Rice with Chicken)

1 chicken, 2½ pounds, cut up
¼ teaspoon saffron
1 onion
1 tablespoon flour
½ teaspoon salt
¼ cup olive oil
¼ pound lean ham or Canadian bacon diced

1 bunch scallions, chopped
1 small can pimientos, drained, diced
2 tablespoons minced parsley
1 bay leaf, crumbled
1 cup long-grain rice
2½ cups chicken broth
Salt to taste

Separate the breast, wings, upper joints, drumsticks, and liver; place remaining parts of chicken in saucepan with 3 cups water, a peeled onion, the saffron, and 1½ teaspoons salt. Boil 30 minutes, strain, measure to make 2½ cups. Meantime, dust tender parts of chicken with flour and ½ teaspoon salt, cook in hot oil until well browned and tender. Add a few slices of onion to oil to prevent spattering. When tender, remove chicken to large casserole, keeping in oven or warm place. Add ham, scallions, pimiento, and parsley to the skillet, cook until scallions are tender; add bay leaf, rice, the chicken broth, boiling hot, and salt to taste. Bring again to the boil, cook over moderately high heat, uncovered, 10 minutes. Stir well, transfer to casserole with chicken, arranging chicken over the top. Cover, let stand 15 to 20 minutes until all liquid is absorbed; or place uncovered in 325° oven for 20 minutes. Makes 6 to 8 servings, enough for 4 persons.

* * *

Valencia is the city of oranges; Alicante, farther south along the coast, is noted for its date palms, which give a heavy, sweet odor to the air, mingling with the intense fragrance of carnations. Alicante, which was established by Hamilcar as a Carthaginian city about 300 B.C., still has an African air, with its white walls and small-windowed houses, the dusty, arid streets, with their tall, waving palms, and a people more dark-skinned and swarthy than to be found elsewhere in Spain. Once it was an important Roman seaport; today its wharves are used mostly by steamers carrying tourists to the nearby Balearic Islands. The arroz which bears the city's name is made with *langostino* and tiny, very sweet artichokes. Even when made with frozen shrimp and frozen artichoke hearts, it is delicious —and different.

ARROZ ALICANTINA (Rice Alicante Style)

1 pound raw shrimp in the shell	2 pimientos, cut in strips
¼ teaspoon saffron	1 cup long-grain rice
1 medium onion, thinly sliced	2½ cups shrimp stock
1 or 2 garlic cloves, crushed	1 teaspoon minced parsley
¼ cup olive oil	1 package frozen artichoke hearts

Shell and devein shrimp; place shells in kettle with 3 cups water and 1½ teaspoons salt, a pinch of orégano or blended herbs for seafood, and saffron, and boil 15 minutes. Strain, measure 2½ cups stock. Sauté the shelled shrimp with onion and garlic in olive oil just until shrimp start to turn pink; remove shrimp. Add pimiento to oil, cook until onion is tender. Add rice, stir to coat rice with oil. Add shrimp stock, boiling hot, and artichoke hearts defrosted just enough to separate. Bring again to the boil, cook uncovered 10 minutes; replace shrimp, cover tightly, keep in warm place 15 to 20 minutes until all liquid is absorbed—or place uncovered in 325° oven. Makes 4 servings.

ALCACHOFAS CON ARROZ (Artichokes with Rice)

1 small onion, chopped	1 package frozen artichoke hearts
¼ cup chopped ham	1 cup long-grain rice
1 garlic clove, minced	2½ cups water
2 pimientos, chopped	1 teaspoon salt
¼ cup olive oil	Lemon slices

Sauté onion, ham, garlic, and pimientos in olive oil until onion is tender. Add artichoke hearts, cover pan, let steam over low heat 2 minutes to defrost partially, so chokes can be broken apart. Add rice, stir to blend. Add water and salt, bring to a boil, cover, cook over low heat 20 minutes until all liquid is absorbed. Serve with lemon slices as garnish. Makes 3 or 4 servings.

ALMEJAS CON ARROZ (Clams with Rice)

¼ cup olive oil
1 large onion, sliced
1 green pepper, diced
1 cup rice
2 cups stock or bouillon
¼ teaspoon saffron

4 tomatoes, peeled, chopped, or 1 medium can (1 pound) peeled tomatoes
1 teaspoon salt
1 can (7 or 8 ounces) minced clams and juice
12 chopped stuffed olives

Sauté onion and green pepper in olive oil until onion is soft. Add rice, stir to glaze, add stock or bouillon, saffron, tomatoes, salt, and clams with juice; bring to a boil, cook uncovered 15 minutes, add chopped olives, cover, let stand in warm place 10 to 15 minutes until all liquid is absorbed and rice fluffy. (Or can be placed in 300° oven.) Makes 4 or 5 servings.

ARROZ A LA MARINERA (Rice Fisherman's Style)

1½ pounds large raw shrimp in shell
¼ teaspoon saffron
¼ cup olive oil
1 pound flounder or halibut, cut in serving pieces
1 tablespoon flour
1 large onion, sliced
2 or 3 garlic cloves, minced

1 small can (3 or 4 ounces) pimientos, drained and diced
1 bay leaf
1 cup rice
2 cups shrimp stock
1 can (7½ ounces) minced clams with juice
Fresh parsley

Shell and devein shrimp, placing shells in saucepan with 2½ cups water and 1½ teaspoons salt, and saffron. Make shrimp stock by boiling shells for 15 minutes, strain. Meantime, sauté shelled shrimp in hot olive oil until bright pink; remove. Dust flounder or halibut in flour, sauté lightly in same oil, remove. Add onion, garlic, pimiento, and bay leaf to oil. Cook over low heat until onion is tender but not browned. Add rice; stir to coat with oil. Replace fish (but not shrimp). Add strained shrimp stock and clams. (Total liquid including juice of clams should be 2½ cups.) Bring to a boil; reduce heat and cook *uncovered* 10 minutes. Replace shrimp, pushing them down into rice mixture, then cover, let stand in warm place 10 to 15 minutes until all liquid is absorbed. Sprinkle with fresh minced parsley before serving. Makes 4 to 6 servings.

ARROZ PRIMAVERA (Springtime Rice)

3 tablespoons olive oil	1 pound fresh asparagus, or 1
1 large onion, thickly sliced	can white asparagus
2 slices bacon, diced	1 cup shelled peas
1 garlic clove, crushed	2½ cups liquid
1 small can (4 ounces)	1½ teaspoons salt
pimientos, drained, diced	¼ teaspoon saffron
1 cup long-grain rice	2 hard-cooked eggs

Cook onion, bacon, and garlic in the olive oil, using large, deep skillet, until onion is transparent and bacon partially cooked. Add pimientos, cook about 30 seconds longer. Add rice, stir to coat with oil. Meantime, separately cook the vegetables in salted water until just tender, still crisp (or if canned asparagus is used, drain, saving liquid). Measure vegetable stock to make 2½ cups, add saffron, bring to a boil, strain. Add this boiling hot to rice, bring again to a boil, cook uncovered 10 minutes, add peas and asparagus, then cover and let stand in warm place 10 to 15 minutes longer until all liquid is absorbed. Serve with asparagus arranged in spokes over rice with quartered eggs in between spears of asparagus. Makes 4 or 5 servings.

ARROZ CON HABAS (Rice with Beans)

2 tablespoons olive oil
1 onion, sliced
10 blanched almonds, coarsely chopped
1 cup long-grain rice

1 teaspoon salt
1 package frozen Fordhook Limas
½ cup chopped black olives
2½ cups boiling water

Sauté onion and almonds in the olive oil until onion is tender. Add rice, stir to coat with olive oil. Add remaining ingredients, bring water again to a boil, cook uncovered 10 to 15 minutes, cover, reduce heat or, if you are using a heavy saucepan with tight cover, turn off heat and let stand 10 to 15 minutes longer until all liquid is absorbed and rice is fluffy. Excellent as an accompaniment to baked ham. Makes 4 to 6 servings.

CHAPTER 7

Carnes

(MEATS)

In Spain, the land of the bullfighters, the beef is not very good. Cows are more valued for their milk; bulls, those with promise, are saved for the ring—and the "moment of truth" does not make their steaks any more tender.

The veal in Spain is, however, excellent—far better than ours. It is used in many of the ways that we use beef, grilled in steaks over charcoal, spit-roasted, pot-roasted in a savory sauce. Veal *filetes* (scallopini) are served up in many wondrous ways.

Suckling lamb is a specialty throughout Castile and in the north, too, in the Basque country. Certain types of lambs are raised especially for meat and these are killed when only twenty-six days old. Even the largest of the lambs in the Spanish markets are tiny by our standards. A suckling lamb will be split in two, and half a baby lamb is enough for just one meal for 2 or 3 persons. It takes 2 "full size" legs of lamb to serve 6 persons adequately. This means that the way of cooking lamb in Spain is far different from ours: because it is so young, it is more often charcoal-grilled than roasted. For that matter, there are few ovens in Spanish kitchens—except in homes of the well-to-do, and most cooking is done over charcoal braziers or stoves with just one or two burners. Fuel is expensive; quick cooking is preferred.

Suckling pig appears on nearly every restaurant menu in Castile and the fragrance of roasting pork is lovely to meet as one enters the restaurant doors. However, I must confess that for my own taste the suckling pig is much too fat, even though the meat is sweet and wonderfully tender. I prefer the lean succulence of pork loin from a full-grown animal. Both pork and ham are used extensively in Spanish cookery, especially in bits and pieces, appearing in bean and rice dishes, *entremeses*, salads, and cooked with vegetables. Baked ham surrounded by *huevos hilado* is an Andalusian specialty: these are thin strands of candied egg yolk, pretty to look at and a delightful flavor complement to the red sweet hams of Spain.

Calf's liver and lamb kidneys pop up frequently, and are deliciously prepared. The liver, especially, is so tender and delicate in flavor it is almost like steak.

A restaurant which nearly every visitor to Madrid goes to at least once is the Casa Botín in the old quarter of Madrid, near the recently renovated Plaza Mayor. The house was founded (Antigua Casa Sobrino de Botín is the full name, but everyone refers to it simply as Casa Botín) in 1725 and the original oven is still used for roasting the suckling lambs and suckling pigs which are its specialties. According to its menu, which is free for the asking, to be carried home as a souvenir, the chefs of Casa Botín are members of the venerable Chaîne des Rôtisseurs brotherhood, founded in 1248. The menu also carries a charming print of old Madrid as it appeared in 1561 and a convenient map of the city's old quarter. The lamb as served at Casa Botín has a most wonderful sauce aromatic of cumin, one that we can use on roasted leg of lamb in the same way.

I'm told that suckling lambs are occasionally to be found in American markets, especially in the Italian quarters of our larger cities around Easter time. In the Pacific Northwest, also, the baby lambs may be found in butcher shops, because there are so many Basques from Spain living in the states of Oregon, Washington, and Wyoming. It's worth a try, for these make wonderful eating.

CORDERO ASADO A LA CASA BOTIN
(Roast Lamb Casa Botín)

Small leg of lamb, 5½ to 6 pounds	*½ teaspoon powdered cumin*
3 to 4 tablespoons olive oil	*¼ teaspoon crushed rosemary*
1 teaspoon paprika	*⅛ teaspoon orégano*
1 garlic clove, crushed	*1 teaspoon salt*
	Lemon wedges

Combine oil, paprika, garlic, cumin, herbs and salt, rub into meat, which should be trimmed of all excess fat. Impale on barbecue spit, roast, turning slowly over moderate fire, until meat thermometer registers 150° (for pink), 25 minutes to the pound. Space briquettes apart to keep fire moderate, or douse occasionally with water, if there is much flaring. Meat should be pink and very tender. Serve lemon wedges with the lamb, sprinkling juice over meat as it is carved. (Or roast lamb in oven at 325°, basting occasionally with pan drippings, for 25 minutes to pound.) Serves 6 to 8 persons.

* * *

Another way of seasoning roast lamb is with a garlic-almond paste, which gives a more pungent flavor.

CORDERITO ASADO A LA CASTELLANA
(Suckling Lamb Roasted in Castilian Style)

Rub one-half a suckling lamb (or a leg of tender young lamb) with salt and pepper, inside and out. Brush all over with olive oil. Mash 2 garlic cloves and 4 toasted almonds in a mortar, add 1 teaspoon paprika and enough red wine to make a thin paste. Impale lamb on spit or on rack above charcoal fire; or in 325° oven. Roast until thermometer inserted in meat (without touching bone) registers 150°; for American lamb, this would be allowing 25 to 30 minutes to the pound. (The Spanish lambs are so young they will be ready to serve much more quickly.) Brush with the garlic paste as it roasts. One half suckling lamb will serve 3 persons. A 6-pound leg of lamb will serve 8 to 10.

* * *

Not far from the Casa Botín, in fact under the archway leading from the Plaza Mayor into the Calle de Cuchilleros, where Casa Botín is located, is another especially fine restaurant, called El Púlpito. Here one sits at white-clothed tables within sight of the friendly kitchen, watching the buxom proprietress as the selected food is cooked to order. A specialty of the house is their *sopa de pescado*—the first are chopped up to be cooked after the order is taken, sizzled in oil in a big black kettle, then simmered in rich dark fish stock which finally is thickened to a cream with mashed egg yolk. While you enjoy the soup, a rack of lamb may be grilled over charcoal, its sizzling brown fragrance wafting out from the kitchen. The grilled lamb is sliced into chops with swift strokes, each chop containing perhaps one good bite. Tender young lamb like this really needs no other seasoning than salt and pepper, although, because the lambs are so young and lacking in fat, the meat is usually brushed with oil to brown it more quickly and evenly.

* * *

Another way of flavoring roast lamb is to insert strips of ham, "buttered" with a garlic paste, into the meat before grilling. This is a specialty of Andalusia.

MECHADA DE CORDERO (Larded Lamb)

1 leg of lamb, 6 to 7 pounds
2 thin slices of ham
1 teaspoon salt
1 tablespoon minced parsley
1 peppercorn
1 or 2 garlic cloves
2 tablespoons olive oil

Combine salt, parsley, peppercorn, and garlic, mash to a paste with mortar and pestle. Blend in olive oil; spread this mixture over the ham. Cut the ham into thin slivers. Cut gashes in the lamb with a small, sharp knife, force the ham strips into the holes. Brush the meat all over with olive oil and roast in an oven at 325° until a meat thermometer registers 150° (pink), about 25 minutes to the pound; or barbecue on a rotating spit over charcoal or in a rotisserie. Serves 8 to 10.

CALDERETA DE CORDERO AL JEREZ
(Lamb Stew, Jerez Style)

2½ pounds lamb for stew
½ cup vinegar
½ cup water
1 or 2 garlic cloves
3 tablespoons olive oil
1½ teaspoons salt
¼ teaspoon freshly ground
   black pepper
⅛ teaspoon powdered cloves
1 tablespoon flour
2 medium onions, sliced
1 cup boiling water
2 tablespoons dry sherry
1 tablespoon fresh mint,
   chopped fine, or 1 teaspoon
   dried mint

Marinate meat about 1 hour in equal parts vinegar and cold water, turning once or twice; drain, pat dry. Place peeled garlic clove in the olive oil, heat until garlic is lightly browned, then remove. Rub the meat in mixture of salt, pepper, cloves, and flour; brown in the hot oil until crisp, then push to one side of pan. Cook onions over moderate heat until soft; replace meat, add boiling water, stir until smooth. Cover, cook gently until tender, 2 to 3 hours, adding sherry during last half hour. Crush fresh mint to a paste with mortar and pestle, blend with a little meat gravy, add to remaining gravy. Or rub dried mint between fingers, add direct to gravy. *Do not add mint until last 5 minutes!* Depending on amount of bone and fat, makes 4 to 6 servings.

COCHIFRITO (Fricassee of Lamb with Artichokes)

2 to 3 pounds lamb cut for stew
Seasoned flour
3 to 4 tablespoons olive oil
1 garlic clove
1 tablespoon minced parsley
1 teaspoon paprika

Juice ½ lemon
1 cup water
1 tablespoon instant minced onion
1 package frozen artichoke hearts

Carefully cut away fat and muscular tissue; cut meat into cubes. Roll in seasoned flour. Place whole garlic clove in oil, heat until garlic is brown, then remove. Brown floured meat in oil until brown on all sides; push to one side of pan. Add parsley and paprika, cook a few seconds, then add lemon juice and water. Cover, simmer until lamb is tender, about 1 hour. During last 10 minutes add artichoke hearts, cook until they are tender. Delightful flavor combination! Depending on amount of bone and fat in meat, makes 6 to 8 servings.

CHULETAS DE CORDERO CON ALI-OLI
(Lamb Chops with Ali-oli Sauce)

Have loin or rib chops cut 1 inch thick, grill under broiler or over charcoal until succulently browned on both sides, taking care not to overcook. Spoon *ali-oli* sauce (see Index) over chops as they are taken from the grill to melt into a golden garlicky stream over the sizzling meat.

CORDERO A LA CHILINDRON (Lamb Chilindrón)

A touch of Moorish influence is apparent in this lamb stew spiced with cinnamon.

¼ cup olive oil	1 large can (1 pound 14
1½ pounds lean boned lamb,	ounces) tomatoes
cut in cubes	1½ teaspoons salt
¾ cup diced onion	Dash of black pepper
1 garlic clove, minced	½ bay leaf
1½ cups diced green pepper	½ teaspoon cinnamon
	½ cup bread in small cubes

Heat olive oil in heavy skillet, add lamb, sauté until browned on all sides. Add onions, garlic, and green pepper, cook over moderate heat 5 minutes; add tomatoes, bring to a boil, simmer gently for 10 minutes. Add remaining ingredients, cook, uncovered, 15 minutes. Meantime, sauté bread crumbs separately in 2 additional tablespoons olive oil. Serve lamb topped with sautéed crumbs. Makes 4 to 6 servings.

MENESTRA DE CORDERO LEVANTINA
(Lamb Stew Levantine Style)

2 pounds boneless lean lamb,	1 cup chicken bouillon
cut in cubes	1 cup white wine
¼ cup olive oil	Salt to taste
1 garlic clove	1 pound fresh peas, or ½
6 small white onions, peeled	package frozen peas
2 carrots, in small cubes	1 package frozen artichoke
3 or 4 tomatoes, peeled and	hearts or frozen Limas
chopped, or 1 cup tomato	
sauce	

Sauté the cubed lamb in olive oil in a skillet until browned on all sides. Place the whole garlic clove in the oil until well browned, then remove and discard. Remove lamb to casserole. Add onions to skillet, cook until nicely brown; remove to casserole. Add carrots, tomatoes, bouillon, and wine to skillet. Bring to a boil, cook until all brown bits in bottom of skillet have been absorbed, about 3 minutes; taste for seasoning, add salt as needed, pour over lamb in casserole. Complete cooking in oven (350°), for 1 hour, or on top of stove, covered, over very low heat until tender. Add shelled peas and artichoke hearts during last 15 minutes. Makes 8 servings, enough for 4 to 6 persons.

One of the most memorable meals we enjoyed during our visit to Spain was in a tiny, modest restaurant in the town of Berriz, not far from Bilbao, in north Spain. We would never have thought of stopping there if Frank Howell, the TWA manager in Madrid, had not recommended the Casa Julian-chu. In fact, our chauffeur had to drive around the town asking where the restaurant was located.

We were returning to San Sebastián from Santander when we came to Berriz, a drive over richly beautiful mountains which rise from the Atlantic in regal splendor. The road wound on the precipice, often so sharp above the sea we could look right down to the water splashing on the rocks far below. Every now and then long, crescent-shaped beaches would appear where fjord-like inlets reached in between the high hills; this is a favorite summer resort area, for while rainfall is high, the temperature is always moderate, even in midsummer. Santander draws hundreds of French visitors every summer, San Sebastián is more popular with English tourists. Throughout the coastal region there are many famous restaurants and food standards are exceptionally high.

When our chauffeur had located Casa Julianchu, it was clear that he was puzzled by our choice, for the place was neither famous nor impressive in appearance. It was a Sunday, and we walked in through the bar, which was so jammed with men having *aperitivos* we could scarcely make our way to the dining room. In fact, in order to reach the dining room it was necessary to walk through the kitchen, a spotlessly clean room where kettles were simmering on a white stove. Frank had told us to order steaks at Julianchu, and we did so—after finding a French-speaking native to interpret our desires. "*Chuletas,*" we heard him explain. My daughter, growing impatient while we waited for our meal to be cooked, wandered out to a small porch where a charcoal grill was being fanned up, and she watched in fascination as the proprietor-cook grilled enormous veal steaks, nearly three inches thick, reporting to me on the progress of our meal as the odor of grilled meat began to float into the dining room.

Meantime, we were served a simple but absolutely perfect chicken consommé with tiny, tiny noodles floating in it. With the steaks we had brown-crusted potatoes and a salad, again simple but perfect. The greens were so crisp and fresh, the dressing nothing more than perfect oil and fresh, aromatic vinegar, with a touch of sliced onion for sweetening—this is salad as salad should be. The dessert, too, was memorable: homemade ice cream, smooth and fragrant of vanilla, a spongecake roll with a date filling, its top golden with tender meringue. The recipe for the cake appears in the *postres* chapter as *merengue de tarta a la Julianchu.*

CHULETAS DE TERNERA A LA JULIANCHU
(Charcoal-Grilled Veal Steaks)

The Spanish veal is so tender and juicy, it can be placed right over charcoal for grilling. However, our American veal tends to be too dry for this: it is better to marinate it first before placing over charcoal. It must be that the calves in Spain are younger when butchered than ours, for the meat was cooked rare, and it was delicious, yet American veal needs to be cooked longer, with added moisture, and should be well done.

2 rump chops of veal, 1½ inches thick
½ cup olive oil
1 teaspoon lemon juice
2 garlic cloves, crushed
¼ teaspoon orégano
¼ cup white wine
Freshly ground black pepper

Punch holes in the meat with a heavy barbecue skewer; combine remaining ingredients, brush over meat, forcing liquid of marinade into the holes. Let stand in marinade at room temperature for at least 1 hour. Place over hot coals of barbecue grill, 4 inches from heat, or under preheated broiler, cook until well browned, basting occasionally with marinade, allowing approximately ½ hour for each side. Fire should not be too hot; space briquettes farther apart to slow the grilling, or, if there is much flaring, sprinkle water over the flames. The steaks will be large—each should make 2 servings. Trying it back home (only 1½ rather than 3 inches thick), we agreed that this was wonderfully sweet meat, completely different barbecue fare.

TERNERA CAZUELA (Veal in Casserole)

Rump of veal, about 4 pounds
3 tablespoons olive oil
1 medium onion, coarsely chopped
2 garlic cloves, minced
1 pimiento, chopped
2 tablespoons flour
1½ teaspoons salt
½ cup white wine
2 cups boiling water
1 tablespoon tomato catsup
1 green pepper, seeded, cut in half

Sauté onion, garlic, and pimiento in oil until soft; remove, purée in blender or crush with back of spoon to a paste. Meantime, flour the meat, brown the meat in the same oil. Add the wine and catsup to the vegetable purée, return to casserole with meat. Add boiling water and salt and the green pepper. Cover casserole, cook over very low heat 3 to 4 hours or until tender. Serves 4 to 6 persons.

TERNERA SALTEADA AL JEREZ
(Veal Scallopini in Sherry Sauce)

12 *veal scallopini*	½ *cup very dry sherry*
2 *tablespoons flour*	1 *cup chicken consommé*
1 *teaspoon salt*	⅛ *teaspoon thyme*
3 *or 4 tablespoons olive oil*	¼ *teaspoon basil*
2 *large onions*	*Salt and pepper to taste*
4 *tablespoons butter, or 2 of*	*Chopped toasted almonds*
butter and 2 of olive oil	2 *tablespoons oloroso sherry*

Pound flour blended with salt into scallopini using the edge of a saucer. Sauté until golden brown in olive oil. Separately sauté onions in butter and oil, slowly, until tender but not brown. Place scallopini over onions. Add sherry, chicken consommé, herbs, salt and pepper. Simmer very gently for about 40 minutes or until scallopini are tender. Serve topped with chopped almonds and sprinkle oloroso sherry over top at last minute. Serves 6 persons.

In Seville they have a dish called *pulpetas*, which turn out to be astonishingly like what we call "veal birds." On the island of Mallorca, a similar dish is called *perdices del capellán*, literally "partridges of the chaplain." The monasteries have been the source of many of the world's great dishes; this apparently is another of clerical inspiration.

PERDICES DEL CAPELLAN (Mock Partridges)

6 slices veal scallopini
6 slices thin ham to match
6 slices salami
1 tablespoon each butter and
    olive oil
2 garlic cloves

1 teaspoon mixed dried herbs,
    such as orégano, thyme,
    basil
½ teaspoon salt
Freshly ground pepper
½ cup white wine
1 cup boiling-hot bouillon

With the edge of a saucer pound the veal slices until very
thin. Cut the ham slices to fit over the veal, and pound the
edges of the two meats together with a mallet or hammer (well
scrubbed). Fit the slice of salami over the ham. Roll up the
"birds" and fasten with toothpicks or tie with thread. Dust
with flour, sauté until golden in a mixture of the oil and butter,
along with the peeled garlic cloves (remove these when
browned) and the herbs. When nicely browned on all sides,
add the salt and pepper, wine, and bouillon. Simmer gently
30 minutes, reducing sauce. 6 servings.

PULPETAS (Veal Birds)

STUFFING

1 cup chopped cooked ham
1 cup minced mushrooms
2 hard-cooked eggs, chopped
⅓ cup chopped pimiento-
    stuffed olives
2 small garlic cloves, crushed
¼ cup minced parsley
Pinch of nutmeg
½ teaspoon salt
1 egg, beaten
½ cup fine bread crumbs

PULPETAS

6 thin slices veal from leg, each
    about 6 by 6 inches
¼ cup olive oil
1 medium can (1 pound) to-
    matoes
1 tablespoon instant minced
    onion
¼ cup medium dry sherry
½ teaspoon salt

Combine ham, mushrooms, chopped eggs, olives, garlic, parsley, nutmeg, and ½ teaspoon salt. Blend thoroughly, add egg and crumbs, blend again, divide into 6 portions. Use as stuffing for the veal slices, which should be pounded and flattened with the edge of a saucer until very thin. Roll up slices, fasten with toothpicks, brown on all sides in the olive oil. Remove to casserole, add to pan in which veal was browned the tomatoes, onion, sherry, and salt. Cook, stirring up browned bits from bottom, until well blended. Pour over *pulpetas* in uncovered casserole. Bake at 350° for 1 hour. Makes 6 servings.

CHULETAS DE TERNERA CAPRICHO
(Veal Chops Caprice)

4 *thick loin veal chops*	3 *to 4 tablespoons olive oil*
2 *tablespoons flour*	1 *small white onion, minced*
½ *teaspoon salt*	1 *tablespoon minced parsley*
⅛ *teaspoon coarsely ground*	½ *cup chicken broth*
pepper	4 *slices Gruyère cheese*

Trim chops, cutting off excess fat and end strips of meat. Rub flour, salt and pepper into meat. Sauté in oil until golden on each side; remove to shallow casserole. Add minced onion and parsley to pan and ½ cup chicken broth (½ teaspoon powdered concentrate and ½ cup water). Bring to a boil, cook until onion is tender. Pour broth over chops. Lay slices of cheese over chops. Place in preheated 400° oven until cheese is melted. Serve at once. (Chops can be sautéed in advance, with broth poured over and cheese placed on meat. Twenty minutes before serving, turn on oven to reheat until cheese is melted and bubbly.) A specialty of the Castellana Hilton Hotel in Madrid. Serves 4.

ESCALOPES DE TERNERA CON CALABACINES
(Veal Scallopini with Zucchini)

12 *thin scallopini slices of veal*
1 *tablespoon flour*
½ *teaspoon salt*
2 *tablespoons milk*
1 *egg, well beaten*
2 *tablespoons fine dry crumbs*
2 *tablespoons butter*

1 *tablespoon olive oil*
Juice ½ *lemon*
2 *small zucchini squash, thinly sliced*
2 *to 3 tablespoons very dry sherry*

Pound flour and salt into veal slices with edge of plate, making veal as flat as possible. Dip in milk blended with egg, then in crumbs. Heat butter and oil until butter is melted, sauté veal over moderate heat until golden on both sides. Remove veal to platter. In same pan, cook squash until tender and slightly browned. Squeeze lemon over veal and zucchini. Add sherry to pan in which veal and squash cooked, increase heat, cook until browned bits have been loosened and "deglazed," making a thin brown bubbling sauce. Pour this sauce over veal and squash. Serves 6.

TERNERA CON NARANJA (Veal in Orange Sauce)

4-*pound rump of veal*
3 *tablespoons flour*
1 *teaspoon salt*
2 *tablespoons olive oil*
1 *medium onion, chopped*
1 *clove garlic, minced*

⅓ *cup orange juice*
Grated rind 1 orange
¼ *teaspoon cinnamon*
¼ *cup chopped hazelnuts*
½ *cup amontillado sherry*
1 *cup water*

Blend flour and salt together, rub into meat. Brown meat in olive oil in skillet over high heat until crisp on all sides. Remove meat to casserole. Add onion and garlic with additional oil as needed, cook until soft but not brown; add orange juice, grated rind, cinnamon, nuts, and sherry. Bring to a boil, lower heat, cook 1 minute. Pour sauce over meat in casserole, add water, cover, simmer over lowest heat 2 hours; or place covered in 300° oven for 2 hours, uncover, bake 15 minutes longer. Remove meat from casserole; skim off excess fat from sauce, thicken sauce with a paste of 1 teaspoon cornstarch thinned in a little water, cooking until sauce is thickened and translucent. Serve sauce with meat. Depending on cut of meat, size and position of bone, makes about 6 servings.

A most elegant small restaurant in Seville is Los Corales on the Paseo Sierpes. The dining room, typically, is on the second floor, and here in an atmosphere of quiet luxury one is served superbly cooked food. The night I was there, three famous movie stars were also in the room, each dining with his own party: Alec Guinness, Anthony Quinn, and Claude Rains. They were in Seville for the filming of *Lawrence of Arabia*. (Seville's alcazar was being used as the backdrop for an Arabian palace, while local gypsies had been taken on as extras, I was told, wearing burnooses to resemble Arabs.) I was interested to overhear Anthony Quinn pronounce this the best restaurant in Seville, for I had already come to the same conclusion. As an entree, I chose *escalope zingara*, whose recipe I have reconstructed according to taste as faithfully as possible.

ESCALOPE ZINGARA (Veal Scallopini Gypsy Style)

12 *veal scallopini*
¼ *cup flour*
¾ *teaspoon salt*
2 *tablespoons butter*
2 *tablespoons olive oil*
2 *tablespoons chopped onion*
½ *green pepper, minced*
½ *cup minced ham*
¼ *pound mushrooms, minced*
¼ *cup oloroso sherry*
1 *cup water*
1 *teaspoon cornstarch*
Salt to taste

Pound the veal with flour and salt until worked in thoroughly, using edge of saucer. Heat the butter and olive oil in a skillet until butter is melted, sauté the scallopini quickly until lightly browned. Remove to shallow casserole or copper baking dish. Add onion, pepper, ham, and mushrooms to skillet; cook until tender and lightly browned. Place a mound of this mixture over each scallopini. Add the sherry to the skillet, increase heat, bring sherry to boil, then add water, stirring to loosen all browned bits from bottom of pan. Simmer until sauce is reduced. Make a thin paste of the cornstarch and some of the sauce, add to the sauce, simmer until slightly thickened. Pour this over the scallopini. Complete cooking scallopini in preheated 325° oven for 30 minutes. Makes 6 servings.

* * *

For the benefit of American and British tourists, many of the luxury restaurants and hotels in Spain now buy steaks of prize steers, animals raised in Spain of pedigreed stock especially for the tourist trade and the more cosmopolitan Spaniards who have developed a taste for beefsteak. The Spanish word for such steaks is *solomillo*, though the word sometimes is applied to veal and even pork steaks, too. The international terms *tournedos* and *filet mignon* will also be found. A tournedos is cut usually from the small end of the filet mignon and is the tenderest of all individual steaks. Those we had at the Palace Hotel in Madrid were butter-tender. Here is a fancy way of preparing *filete* as served at the Castellana Hilton. If your pocketbook does not allow filet mignon, try this with choice quality sirloin.

FILETE GREDOS (*Fillet of Beef Gredos*)

Ask your butcher to cut filet mignon or sirloin into individual steaks 1 inch thick, then cut a pocket in the center of each. Force a spoonful of well-seasoned liver *pâté* in the center of each. Heat 2 tablespoons each butter and olive oil in a heavy skillet, sauté the steaks quickly over high heat until well browned on each side, allowing 3 minutes per side for rare. Remove steaks to hot plates, sauté mushroom caps in the same skillet, place a mushroom cap on top of each steak. Add 2 or 3 spoonfuls of cream sherry to the pan, cook to deglaze the brown bits of meat crust on the bottom, then pour this essence over the steak. Serve accompanied by asparagus spears.

* * *

Even a tough cut of meat can be tender and flavorful with this treatment. The lemon and orange give the beef delightful zest.

CADERA DE TORO (Bullfighter's Steak)

3-pound "bargain" chuck steak	2 cloves garlic
½ cup olive oil	2 whole cloves
1 lemon, quartered	1 bay leaf
½ orange, quartered	

Place lemon, orange, whole peeled garlic, whole cloves, and bay leaf in olive oil, heat until rind of fruit is brown, strain, discard. Pierce meat with heavy skewer all over, then pour strained hot oil over meat, marinate 4 hours or longer at room temperature. Remove meat from marinade, place in very hot heavy skillet, sear quickly, then turn heat as low as possible, cook about 20 minutes on each side for rare, 25 to 30 minutes on each side for medium. Meat should be browned on outside, still tender and pink on inside. Serve with *ali-oli* sauce (see Index). Depending on amount of bone and fat in cut, makes about 4 to 6 servings.

ESTOFADO DE VACA (Beef Pot Roast)

Rump of beef (chuck) 3 to 4 pounds
¼ teaspoon marjoram
2 bay leaves, crushed
1 garlic clove, crushed
1 green pepper, minced
1 small onion, minced

4 tablespoons Spanish olive oil
1 medium can (1 pound) tomatoes
¼ teaspoon cinnamon
⅛ teaspoon cloves
2 cups red wine
2 teaspoons salt or to taste

Combine marjoram, bay leaves, garlic, green pepper, and onion, mash to paste in mortar with olive oil, rub into beef top and bottom. Let stand 1 hour. Sear beef in heated pot-roast kettle until well browned, add remaining ingredients, cover, simmer gently 3 or 4 hours until tender. Remove meat from kettle, thicken sauce if desired with 1 tablespoon cornstarch, cooking until smooth and shiny. Serve sliced meat with the sauce. Depending on cut of meat and amount of bone and fat, makes about 6 servings.

Note: Instead of simmering in a kettle, meat may be wrapped in a double thickness of aluminum foil large enough to hold all the ingredients, then sealed tightly and cooked in the oven at 375°. In this case, reduce wine to ½ cup.

* * *

Dishes with names like "drunken pig," "soused veal," and "tipsy chicken" can be found in the culinary repertoires of most wine-drinking countries. It amuses cooks apparently to think of their victims simmering in a wine sauce as they are readied for the table—what better way to be prepared for the afterlife? The beef in this Spanish recipe is "drunk" with Spanish sherry.

CARNE BORRACHA (Intoxicated Beef)

1½ pounds lean stewing beef, cubed
2 tablespoons olive oil
1 tablespoon butter
1 teaspoon salt
⅛ teaspoon powdered cloves
¼ teaspoon cumin
1 tablespoon minced parsley
¼ cup raisins
6 pimiento-stuffed olives
1 cup very dry Spanish sherry

Heat oil and butter until butter is melted, add beef, brown on all sides. Add salt and spices, parsley, raisins, olives, and sherry. Cover, cook gently over lowest heat until meat is tender, about 1 hour. Add water if necessary, if liquid cooks away. Serve over bed of hot cooked rice. Makes 4 servings (but for gourmets, this will serve only 2 persons).

CADERA DE VACA A LA CASTELLANA
(Beef Pot Roast Castilian Style)

In Spain this would be simmered gently in a kettle for hours, but the American method of pot-roasting in foil in the oven is far superior.

3½-to-4-pound boned, rolled chuck roast, fat removed
¼ teaspoon black pepper
¼ teaspoon dried tarragon
½ teaspoon grated lemon peel
1 teaspoon paprika
1 or 2 garlic cloves, crushed
2 tablespoons olive oil

If selecting meat at your butcher's, instruct that it be rolled without any covering of suet. If you buy at the supermarket and the roast is already wrapped with suet, be sure to remove and discard it. Pierce meat with large skewer, combine seasonings and oil, and pour over the holes so oil will penetrate through meat. Place meat in center of large sheet of aluminum foil (I prefer to use a double thickness of foil), seal foil securely by crimping edges. Place in roasting pan in oven set at 250°; roast 4 to 5 hours. No liquid need be added; when foil is unwrapped, you will find at least a cup of deliciously flavored sauce. Strain sauce, pour into saucepan, skim off excess fat, thicken slightly with paste of flour or cornstarch, and add salt to taste. Simmer 10 minutes. Serve sliced meat with sauce. Makes 10 to 12 servings; for company, serves to 6 persons.

CHULETAS DE CERDO A LA ARAGONESA
(Pork Chops Aragonese Style)

6 *lean pork chops*	1 *teaspoon salt*
1 *small garlic clove, crushed*	½ *cup chopped onion*
1 *teaspoon paprika*	1 *tomato, peeled and chopped*
Pinch of *powdered cloves*	2 *tablespoons vinegar*
¼ *cup olive oil*	1 *cup water or stock*
2 *tablespoons flour*	Pinch of *saffron*

Mash together garlic, paprika, cloves, and olive oil. Rub into chops, let stand several hours or overnight. When ready to cook, lift from marinade, dust with the flour blended with salt. Add a tablespoon of the oil to a heated skillet, "roll" to cover bottom, then add floured chops and brown quickly. Remove when browned, add chopped onion to the pan, cook until tender (add some of the marinade if more fat is needed); add tomato, cook to a mush. Add vinegar, water or stock, and saffron, bring to a boil, reduce heat; replace chops in the sauce, simmer until tender, about 25 minutes. 6 servings.

LOMO TRUFADO CON CHAMPINONES
(Loin of Pork with Mushroom Stuffing)

4 *thick pork chops*	2 *tablespoons flour*
¼ *cup minced mushrooms*	½ *teaspoon salt*
1 *tablespoon minced onion*	Olive *oil*
2 *tablespoons minced green pepper*	2 *tablespoons brandy*
Pinch of *cumin*	1 *cup chicken bouillon*
¼ *teaspoon salt*	¼ *cup raisins*

Cut a pocket in the center of each pork chop. Combine mushrooms, onion, green pepper, cumin, and ¼ teaspoon salt, insert a little of mixture into each chop. Dust chops with flour and salt, sauté in olive oil until crisply brown. Drain off all fat, add brandy, set aflame. When flame has died out, add chicken bouillon and raisins, simmer until chops are tender, about 35 minutes. (If desired, thicken sauce with a little cornstarch, simmering until smooth.) Serves 4.

CHULETAS CON SALSA DE TOMATES
(Pork Chops in Tomato Sauce)

Sauté either pork or veal chops in olive oil; remove, make tomato sauce (see Index), using onions, garlic, pimiento, tomato, and seasonings. Return chops to pan along with a dozen sliced stuffed olives, simmer until chops are tender, about 35 minutes.

PICADILLO (Hash)

4 tablespoons olive oil	1½ cups chopped cooked
1 medium onion, chopped	pork or veal
1 green pepper, diced	⅛ teaspoon marjoram or
1 ripe tomato, peeled,	orégano
chopped	¼ teaspoon salt

Cook onions, green pepper, and tomato in olive oil until onion is soft. Add meat, stir once or twice with fork until meat is heated through and lightly browned. Serve over hot rice. Makes 3 or 4 servings.

Note: Any leftover meat can be used, beef, veal, or lamb, ham or pork. Even a 12-ounce can of "luncheon meat," believe it or not, will taste good when fixed this way: cut the canned meat into small chunks. It's the olive oil that makes the difference in flavor—don't try to substitute any other oil or fat.

* * *

The art of cooking kidneys is one utterly unknown to most American cooks. In fact, the very word "kidney" creates such consternation when suggested to most Americans that they refuse even to touch the meat. This is sad. Kidneys, when properly prepared, can be sublime in flavor, tender and succulent. I urge you to forget prejudices and try this dish.

RINONES DE CORDERO A LA SENORITA
(Lamb Kidneys)

12 lamb kidneys	¼ teaspoon orégano
2 tablespoons butter	½ teaspoon salt
1 tablespoon olive oil	1 tablespoon minced parsley
2 tablespoons minced onion	½ cup very dry sherry
12 large mushroom caps	¼ cup dry red wine
	Snippets of toast

Slice kidneys crosswise—they should be very fresh, just taken from the fat. Sauté in the butter and oil until lightly brown, taking care not to crowd the pan. Remove as they brown. Add the minced onion and mushroom caps, brown the mushrooms lightly. Add seasonings and wine, replace kidneys, cook quickly over moderately high heat until sauce is reduced and thickened, not more than 4 minutes. (Longer cooking toughens the kidneys and destroys the delicate flavor—then they must be cooked another hour to become tender again.) Serve over snippets of toast as a supper entree to discriminating guests. Serves 4 to 6.

JAMON ASADO CON HUEVOS HILADO
(Baked Ham with Candied Egg Yolk)

This is such a typical and unique Spanish delicacy I felt it should be included as part of *The Art of Spanish Cooking*, but I must confess my own efforts to make this delicate confection were unsuccessful. I enjoyed ham with *huevos hilado* one night at the Beltrán Domecq home in Jerez, along with glasses of Dry Sack sherry, a memorable combination. Anne Williams de Domecq gave me the recipe; my friend and fellow-cookbook-author Nika Hazelton also has a recipe for *huevos hilado* which she swears is not at all difficult to do. We can't all do everything—I'm just not good at candies or frostings or even at cakemaking. Those who excel in such trickery probably will have better luck than I.

Bake ham in your favorite way. A tenderized "ready to eat" ham needs only to have a little sugar and mustard rubbed over the fat, then slipped into the oven for 10 minutes to the pound. A little sherry basting adds delightful flavor. The cold strands of candied egg are served around the base of the ham, along with maraschino cherries.

HUEVOS HILADO (*Candied Egg Yolk*)

2½ cups water
4 cups sugar
12 egg yolks

In a 12-inch skillet, combine water and sugar, cook until sugar is dissolved—but do not allow it to thicken. Carefully separate egg yolks so that no white comes with them. Nika says they should be beaten until thin and heated in the top of a double boiler for 2 or 3 minutes, then poured from a cup into the syrup. Señora de Domecq says they should be "beaten by hand," then dropped in a long thread into the hot syrup (do not stir), or through a "sieve" with four or five widely spaced holes. Since we have no such sieves among our housewares, a frozen-orange-juice can may be used, with several holes punched in the bottom with an ice pick.

The can (or a measuring cup with spout) should be held over the simmering syrup, 12 inches above the pan, rotating the can or cup so that the thread of egg yolk as it falls in a thin stream will form long strands in the syrup. Cook the first batch of "threads" 3 minutes, remove with slotted spoon to a shallow bowl set in a larger bowl of ice water. Repeat with remaining egg yolks, keeping the syrup always at the simmering point—but do not let it boil. The candied yolks must be chilled at once to harden.

ALBONDIGAS DE LOMO (Pork Meat Balls)

MEAT BALLS

SAUCE

MEAT BALLS	SAUCE
1 pound ground pork	20 blanched almonds, chopped
½ pound ground veal	1 slice bread, cubed
2 slices bread	1 or 2 garlic cloves, crushed
¼ cup tomato sauce	1½ cups chicken bouillon
1 egg	2 tablespoons minced onion
1½ teaspoons salt	2 tablespoons minced parsley
1 teaspoon paprika	¼ cup tomato sauce
3 tablespoons olive oil	Salt to taste

Combine meats. Soak bread in water until soft; squeeze out excess water. Add bread, tomato sauce, egg, salt, and paprika to ground meat, work with fingers until very smooth. Form in 1-inch balls. Sauté in olive oil until lightly browned; remove from pan. Add almonds, bread, and garlic to the same oil, sauté until lightly browned; remove, mash in mortar and pestle until a smooth paste. Dilute with some of chicken bouillon until consistency of heavy cream. Add onion and parsley to oil, cook until onion is soft, add tomato sauce, remaining bouillon, and salt to taste. Replace meat balls in sauce, simmer uncovered 30 minutes. During last 10 minutes stir in almond-garlic paste. Makes 6 to 8 servings.

Each province of Spain has its own way of making *cocido*, the stew of *garbanzos* (chick-peas) and various kinds of meat. In Seville it is made with rice and sweet potatoes and blood sausage along with assorted pork products, and flavored strongly of garlic. No garlic at all is used in the cocido of

Granada, white potatoes appear instead of rice, salami will be used instead of blood sausage, and often rabbit or chicken is added. The cocido of Barcelona is made with *butifarra*, a garlic-flavored sausage which is a specialty of Catalonia. The cocido of Madrid often contains several kinds of sausage, green cabbage, or spinach, and very fine noodles (vermicelli) may be added instead of rice or potatoes. As you can see, cocido may be almost anything you like. The two invariables are chickpeas (garbanzos) and pork (or ham). The meat and garbanzos are removed to a platter, the soup served as a first course, and the meat and vegetables as the entree.

COCIDO (Chick-Pea Stew)

1 can (1 pound) chick-peas
1 pound stewing beef, in 1-inch cubes
¼ cup Spanish olive oil
½ pound chorizo, sliced, or 1 cup chopped ham
1 large onion, chopped
1 cup canned tomatoes

Ham bone or knuckle bone
2 leeks or 6 scallions
2 carrots, cut in 2-inch pieces
1 teaspoon salt, or to taste
1 quart water
½ cup rice or 1 pound sweet potatoes, cut in cubes

Drain chick-peas, saving liquid. Sauté cubed beef in the olive oil until browned on all sides; add chorizo or ham, onion, and drained chick-peas, cook until onion is tender. Add tomatoes, the ham or knuckle bone, chopped leeks or scallions, carrots, water, and salt. Cook, covered, 1 hour. Add more water if needed, so that ingredients are covered with liquid. Add rice or cubed sweet potatoes, cook 20 minutes longer. Makes 8 servings, enough for 4 to 6 persons.

Note: The best brand of canned chick-peas (garbanzos) I have been able to find is called Mare Chiare. This may be found in many Italian-Spanish markets or ordered direct from Antonio Piccini, Grocer, in Brooklyn.

HIGADO A LA ASTURIANA (Liver Asturian Style)

1 *pound calf's or steer's* **liver,** *sliced ½ inch thick*	2 *cups vegetable broth,* **or** *bouillon*
3 *tablespoons flour*	*Dash gravy coloring*
½ *teaspoon salt*	2 *tablespoons lemon juice*
4 *or 5 tablespoons Spanish olive oil*	*Salt to taste*
1 *medium onion, minced*	1 *to 2 tablespoons sugar*

Cut liver in pieces 1½ by 2 inches. Roll in seasoned flour. Sauté onion in half the olive oil until tender; remove. Add more olive oil as needed, sauté floured liver a few pieces at a time over reduced heat, just until delicately browned—avoid overcooking. When liver is all cooked, add 2 tablespoons flour to oil in pan, stir to blend, then slowly add vegetable broth or bouillon cubes and water. Add gravy coloring, lemon juice, salt, and sugar. Replace onions and liver. Simmer over low heat about 3 minutes. If possible, make the day ahead and reheat when needed—it is better the second day. Serve with mashed potatoes, glazed minted carrots, and tomatoes with tarragon dressing. Makes 4 servings.

RINONES A LA NAVARRA (Lamb Kidneys Navarra Style)

18 *trimmed lamb kidneys*	1 *clove garlic, crushed*
12 *slices bacon*	1 *tablespoon minced parsley*
¼ *cup Spanish olive oil*	½ *cup soft white bread crumbs*
1 *teaspoon salt*	
⅛ *teaspoon pepper*	

Cut each lamb kidney in 4 slices. Cut bacon in pieces to conform. Arrange kidney and bacon alternately on skewers, brush with olive oil which has been blended with salt and pepper. Place four inches from heat in broiler oven or over charcoal; cook, turning once, until they start to brown. Meantime, crush garlic and parsley together until paste-like, using mortar and pestle; combine with bread crumbs broken very fine. Roll half-broiled kidneys in crumbs, return to fire, continue to cook until crisp and brown on all sides. Serve with brown-crusted potatoes and broccoli vinaigrette. Serves 6 persons.

SESOS REBOZADOS (Calf's Brains)

2 calf's brains
2 cups water
½ teaspoon salt
2 tablespoons vinegar
2 chopped leeks or 6 chopped scallions
2 tablespoons Spanish olive oil
2 tomatoes, peeled and seeded, or 2 tablespoons tomato paste
1 carrot, grated
1 cup chicken broth (or bouillon cube and water)
4 large mushroom crowns

Parboil brains in water to which salt and vinegar have been added; cook 20 to 30 minutes (the longer time if frozen), turn off heat, let cool in stock. Sauté leeks or scallions in olive oil; add tomato, cook until soft. Add carrot and chicken broth, cook 5 minutes. Force sauce through food mill or sieve or purée in blender. Cook down sauce until reduced and thickened; divide among 4 individual ramekins. Slice brains in half crosswise, place in sauce. Top each with large mushroom crown. Brush with mixture 1 teaspoon each melted butter and olive oil. This part can be done in advance. Shortly before dinner is to be served, place ramekins in preheated 350° oven for 20 minutes. Serve to 4 persons with herb-toasted garlic bread and ensalada valenciana (see Index).

CHAPTER 8

Aves

(BIRDS)

The sight of chickens rotating slowly on spits before glowing "fire walls" or on electric rotisseries is almost as common in the larger Spanish cities as in New York. *"Pollo al ast,"* as this way of roasting chicken is called, has become a Spanish fad. There are even little chicken "bars" where one may step in and consume half a chicken astride a bar stool, instead of nibbling on *tapas* when hunger suddenly becomes overpowering.

Ads also appear in Spanish newspapers urging consumers to grow their own chickens, and many families do, in their own back yards. (They also sometimes raise a single sheep, using it as an inexpensive lawn mower until it is grown and ready for the butcher.) For the most part, the Spanish chickens are scrawnier than ours and less tender, but superior strains of pullets have been imported from the United States both for family-unit chicken raising and for breeders. Plymouth Rock has become a well-known name in Spain, meaning the black-and-white-feathered meat birds of that name, not the famous spot where the Pilgrims landed.

The listing under *Aves* on a restaurant menu includes more than chickens, however. Partridges are much less expensive than chickens in Spain, and are prepared in numerous ways. Canned partridges are even sold widely, costing about a dollar a can. Ducks, too, are prepared in wonderfully good ways. Their ducks are very flavorful, lean, the meat rich and dark. Some, I suspect, are wild ducks, for any huntsman can sell his bag of game to restaurants. Rabbits, pheasants, and tiny, tiny game birds also appear frequently for sale in the open markets as well as being offered in fancy dress on restaurant menus.

Many of the Spanish recipes for partridge can be applied to rock Cornish game hens. I have adapted them to whole chicken breasts, since in our markets today tender, meaty chicken breasts are one of the most economical of all meat buys.

Incidentally, *pollo* refers to a young, tender chicken, *gallina* to a stewing hen. Since the fryers are more common in our markets and often less expensive, I have used fryers in many recipes calling for stewing chickens.

PEPITORIA DE GALLINA (Spicy Chicken Fricassee)

1 3-pound chicken, cut up	2 medium cloves garlic,
1 cup chicken stock	minced
1 tablespoon salted flour	1 tablespoon minced parsley
3 tablespoons olive oil	¼ teaspoon saffron
1 large onion, finely chopped	½ to ¾ teaspoon salt
4 tablespoons chopped	Yolks of 2 hard-cooked eggs
almonds	½ cup slivered cooked ham

Set aside more-tender parts of chicken (legs, thighs, breast, and wings), place neck, back, and giblets in 1½ cups water with ½ teaspoon salt, simmer covered for 30 to 40 minutes to make chicken stock. Meantime, dust remaining pieces with salted flour, sauté in hot olive oil until golden and crisp. To prevent spattering, add a few onion slices to oil. When chicken is browned, remove to casserole, add chopped onions to pan, cook over moderate heat until tender but not browned. Add onion to chicken. In a mortar or wooden salad bowl, pound almonds to a paste with garlic, parsley, and saffron. (This can be done in an electric blender.) Add salt and egg yolks, mash to blend, then moisten with some of oil in skillet and gradually add 1 cup chicken stock. Pour this over chicken in casserole. Bake chicken uncovered at 350° for 30 minutes. During last 5 minutes add ham. Serve with hot cooked rice. Makes 4 servings, with 2 pieces of chicken for each serving.

POLLO RELLENO (Stuffed Chicken)

2 broilers (2 pounds each),
   left whole
Softened butter
¼ cup amontillado sherry

STUFFING:

3 cups cooked rice
¼ cup chopped cooked ham
2 chicken livers, sautéed

6 almonds, blanched, sautéed
1 tablespoon minced parsley
2 tablespoons melted butter

Rub chickens generously with softened butter; dust lightly with salt. Combine all ingredients for the stuffing, chopping the livers and almonds. Fill cavities of the chickens loosely with rice mixture. Arrange chickens in large shallow baking dish. Baste with sherry as they roast in preheated 350° oven for 45 minutes or until drumstick moves easily.

As chickens roast, make stock by cooking necks and giblets in salted water; boil stock down to 1 cup. Combine chicken stock with liquid in casserole after chickens are removed, thickening sauce lightly if preferred. Taste for salt. Serve sauce with roasted stuffed chickens, allowing ½ chicken per serving. Serves 4.

Note: The stuffing is exquisite, but just rubbing chickens with butter, then basting them with sherry is superb, even if no stuffing is placed in the chickens at all.

POLLO A LA ARAGONESA (Chicken Aragon Style)

1 3-pound chicken, cut up	⅛ teaspoon ground cumin
4 medium onions, chopped	1 teaspoon salt
4 tablespoons olive oil	⅛ teaspoon ground coriander
1 cup chicken broth	4 tablespoons light cream
1 cup white wine	1 teaspoon minced parsley

Simmer the onions in olive oil over moderate heat until tender but not brown. Remove from pan with slotted spoon; add chicken pieces, cook until golden but not brown. Meantime, make chicken broth by simmering neck and giblets in 1½ cups water and ½ teaspoon salt, reducing liquid to 1 cup. When chicken is golden, replace onions, add broth, wine, spices, and salt. Cover, cook over very low heat until chicken is very tender, about 30 minutes. Remove chicken. Pour broth and onions into tall narrow container so that excess oil will rise to top (half hour in refrigerator) and can be skimmed or poured off easily. Purée remaining sauce in electric blender or force through sieve or food mill. Return to pan, taste, and, if needed, add additional salt. Simmer about 5 minutes, add cream. Sauce should be slightly thickened and very smooth. Serve chicken covered with the sauce. Sprinkle with minced parsley. Serves 4.

PECHUGAS DE POLLO CON SALSA DE ALMENDRAS
(Chicken Breasts with Almond Sauce)

2 *whole chicken breasts, boned*	½ *tablespoon olive oil*
2 *eggs, beaten*	½ *cup chopped blanched almonds*
1 *teaspoon salt*	2 *tablespoons flour*
⅛ *teaspoon pepper*	1 *cup milk*
½ *cup fine dry crumbs*	¼ *cup cream*
Oil *or fat for deep frying*	½ *teaspoon salt*
1½ *tablespoons butter*	¼ *cup pimiento-stuffed olives*

Cut boned chicken into strips ½ inch wide. Beat together eggs, salt and pepper; dip pieces of chicken in eggs then roll in crumbs. Fry in deep oil (365° for olive oil, 375° for other oil or fat) for 6 or 7 minutes until crisp and golden. Lift from oil, drain on absorbent paper. Meantime, melt butter and oil, add chopped blanched almonds and sauté until lightly browned. Blend in flour, then slowly add milk and cook over low heat, stirring, until thickened and smooth. Season to taste, add olives. Place fried chicken on mound of rice, serve sauce separately. Makes 4 servings.

POLLO FRITO AL JEREZ
(Fried Chicken Marinated in Sherry Sauce)

2 *broilers, each cut in 8 pieces*	1 *teaspoon paprika*
⅓ *cup very dry Spanish sherry*	1 *teaspoon cumin*
¼ *cup olive oil*	1 *or 2 garlic cloves, crushed*
1 *teaspoon lemon juice*	1 *teaspoon honey*
	1 *teaspoon salt*

Arrange cut up chicken in deep bowl; cover with remaining ingredients. Marinate 24 hours. Remove from marinade, dust chicken with seasoned flour, fry until crisp on all sides in olive oil. Or, omit flour, broil marinated drained chicken under broiler or over charcoal. Serves 4 to 6 persons.

POLLO CON NARANJA (Chicken with Oranges)

1 3-pound chicken, cut up	*1 cup orange juice*
1 cup chicken broth	*1 cup chicken broth*
2 tablespoons flour	*½ cup raisins*
1 teaspoon salt	*¼ cup ground almonds*
4 or 5 tablespoons olive oil	*¼ teaspoon cinnamon*
1 small onion, chopped	*⅛ teaspoon cloves*

Use neck, wing tips, back, and giblets to make chicken broth, cooking in 1½ cups water with ¼ teaspoon salt, reducing to 1 cup. Dust remaining pieces of chicken with flour blended with salt; fry in olive oil with chopped onion. When chicken is browned, add remaining ingredients, including strained broth. Cook gently, covered, about 40 minutes until chicken is very tender. Serve with rice. Makes 4 servings.

POLLO A LA JARDINERA (Chicken with Vegetables)

2 3-pound chickens, cut up	*1 small tomato, peeled and*
3 cups chicken stock	*chopped, or 1 teaspoon*
¼ cup flour	*tomato paste*
1 teaspoon salt	*½ tablespoon cornstarch*
¼ cup olive oil	*½ head cauliflower, in small*
2 tablespoons butter	*pieces*
1 medium onion, minced	*1 pound fresh peas, or ½*
2 garlic cloves, minced	*package frozen peas, or 1*
½ cup oloroso sherry	*package frozen artichoke*
	hearts

Separate the backs, necks, and giblets from the other chicken parts, cover with 2 cups water and the liquid drained from the canned asparagus; add ½ teaspoon salt and cook, covered, ½ hour to make chicken stock. Meantime, dust remaining pieces of chicken with blended flour and salt, brown quickly in the hot olive oil and butter until crisp on all sides. Remove to casserole. Add onions and garlic to skillet, cook over low heat in oil until soft. Add tomato and sherry, cook 5 minutes, add strained chicken stock, and cook until onions are very soft. Strain sauce or purée in electric blender until smooth. Thicken with cornstarch, cook until shiny-smooth, stirring occasionally. Pour over chicken in casserole. Separately parboil cauliflower 5 minutes (it should still be crisp). Add with peas or artichoke hearts to chicken in casserole (fresh peas need 5 minutes precooking). Place in oven. One-half hour before dinner is to be served, turn on oven to 350°. Add drained asparagus tips during last 10 minutes. Serves 6 to 8 persons.

POLLO FRITO A LA TENERIFE (Fried Chicken Tenerife)

1 3-pound frying chicken	1 small onion, minced
¼ cup flour	⅛ teaspoon cinnamon
1 teaspoon salt	⅛ teaspoon cloves
½ cup olive oil	2 cups white wine
2 garlic cloves, minced	Salt to taste

Dust chicken pieces in flour blended with salt, fry in olive oil until very brown and crisp. (Place piece of bread or slices of onion in oil to prevent spattering.) Remove chicken to casserole. Pour off all but 2 tablespoons oil. Add garlic, onion, cinnamon, and cloves, cook over moderate heat until onion is soft. Add white wine, simmer 10 minutes. Add salt if needed. Pour over chicken, simmer gently about 20 minutes until chicken is very tender. Serves 4 to 6 persons.

GALLINA A LA SEVILLANA
(Chicken Fricassee, Seville Style)

1 3-pound chicken, cut up	1 or 2 garlic cloves, minced
1 cup chicken stock	2 tomatoes, peeled and
2 tablespoons flour	chopped, or 1 cup canned
1 teaspoon salt	tomatoes
Freshly ground black pepper	1 tablespoon brandy
¼ cup olive oil	¼ cup white wine
2 pimientos, drained, diced	12 large stuffed olives, sliced
1 medium onion, chopped	

Separate backs, necks, and giblets from rest of chicken, cover with water, a little salt, simmer ½ hour to make 1 cup stock. Meantime, dust remaining pieces of chicken with flour blended with 1 teaspoon salt and the black pepper; sauté in olive oil until well browned on all sides. (Add 1 or 2 onion slices to oil to prevent spattering.) When browned, remove to casserole; pour off excess oil from skillet, leaving no more than 2 tablespoons, add pimientos, onion, and garlic, cook until vegetables are soft. Add tomatoes, brandy, white wine, and the strained chicken stock. Taste for salt, add more if needed. Simmer until well blended and puréed. Replace chicken in sauce, add olives, simmer uncovered 15 minutes longer. Makes 4 servings.

PECHUGAS DE POLLO A LA CATALANA
(Chicken Breasts Catalan Style)

4 chicken breasts, boned	4 small carrots
1 tablespoon flour	4 leeks
¾ teaspoon salt	½ cup vegetable stock
2 tablespoons olive oil	1 teaspoon cornstarch
2 tablespoons butter	½ cup white wine

Dust chicken breasts with flour and salt, sauté until golden and tender in olive oil and butter. Separately cook carrots (peeled, sliced in half lengthwise) and leeks in salted water until just tender, about 5 minutes. Remove vegetables from liquid (saving stock). Arrange chicken breasts in casserole surrounded by vegetables. Thicken vegetable stock with cornstarch, add to skillet in which chicken breasts were browned. Cook until all browned bits are loosened from pan and sauce is slightly thickened. Pour over chicken and vegetables in casserole, cover, cook over very low heat about 20 minutes. Serve from casserole. Serves 4 persons.

The following delicious way of preparing chicken we enjoyed in San Sebastián, in the Restaurant Eguía in San Sebastián's old quarter, located on a street so narrow the high-topped old taxi could scarcely squeeze between its curbstones. Inside everything was sparkling clean, the waitresses wearing starched aprons, the tablecloths snowy, the walls freshly painted. Every morsel of food, from soup to dessert, was exquisite, and beautifully presented. The name *chilindrón* means a game of cards. The dish, we might say, is a neat trick.

POLLO CHILINDRON (Chicken Chilindrón)

1 *small broiler-fryer, cut up*
2 *tablespoons butter*
1 *tablespoon olive oil*
1 *lean pork chop*
1 *medium onion, chopped fine*
1 *small can pimientos,*
   drained, diced
1 *tablespoon tomato purée or*
   catsup

½ *cup dry white wine*
Pinch each of fennel, marjo-
   ram, and thyme
½ *cup chicken broth*
Salt to taste
1 *small jar artichoke hearts,*
   well drained, or 1 package
   frozen artichoke hearts

Heat butter and oil until well blended, add chicken, brown over moderate heat until golden on all sides. Remove. Cut meat of pork chops from bone, discarding fat and bone; dice remaining meat. Sauté in oil in skillet until brown; add to chicken. Cook onions and pimiento in pan until soft, adding more oil and butter if necessary. Add tomato purée, wine, herbs, chicken broth, and salt to taste. Simmer until well blended, then replace chicken and pork, add artichoke hearts, and simmer 15 minutes. If thickened sauce is desired, make a small ball of butter and flour worked together, add to sauce in pan during last 5 minutes, cook until smooth. Makes 4 or 5 servings.

POLLO AL AST (Chicken on a Spit)

Usually the chickens, broiler size, are simply brushed with olive oil blended with salt and paprika and spit-roasted until golden and tender. For variation, however, here are some interesting marinades, also to be used as basting sauces.

Cumin-glazed: Combine ¼ cup olive oil, 1½ tablespoons vinegar, 2 teaspoons powdered cumin, 1 or 2 crushed garlic cloves, 2 tablespoons honey, and 1 teaspoon salt. Beat to blend well, brush over chicken an hour, at least, before spit-roasting.

Orange Marinade: Grated rind and juice of 1 orange, 1 tablespoon grated onion, ¼ teaspoon cinnamon, ⅛ teaspoon cloves, 1 teaspoon salt, ¼ cup olive oil. Brush chicken inside and out, spoon at least a tablespoon of the marinade inside the cavity of the chicken. Impale on spit and roast in the usual way.

Almond: Blanch and crush 15 to 20 almonds (easy to crush in electric blender), combine with 1 crushed garlic clove or ½ teaspoon garlic powder, ½ teaspoon salt, and the grated rind of ½ lemon. Add oil to make a thin paste. Brush all over outside of chicken, let stand at least ½ hour. Brush some of the marinade over the chicken as it roasts.

GALLINA A LA BILBAINA (Chicken Bilbao Style)

1 5-pound stewing chicken, whole or cut up	1½ cups water
2 to 3 tablespoons olive oil	1 package frozen peas or 2 pounds fresh peas
1 tablespoon salt	1 package frozen artichoke hearts
12 small whole new potatoes, peeled	2 tablespoons flour
2 carrots, quartered	

If chicken is to be cooked whole, place 1 medium onion in cavity, truss as for roasting. Brush chicken with olive oil, place in large, heavy pot, add salt, cover, turn heat low, and steam chicken in oil for 1 hour (chicken should not brown). Add potatoes and carrots, cover again, continue cooking over low heat 30 minutes longer so that juice of chicken penetrates vegetables. Add water, bring to boil, then turn heat low and cook slowly about 40 minutes longer or until chicken is very tender. Add peas and artichokes, cook until tender, about 7 minutes. Skim fat from top of sauce. Mix flour with liquid from pot to make thin paste, stir this into sauce and cook until sauce is smooth and thickened. Serve vegetables with chicken on large platter. Makes 10 to 12 servings.

GALLINA EN CAZUELA AL JEREZ
(Chicken Casserole, Sherry Sauce)

1 frying chicken, cut up	2 garlic cloves, crushed
½ to ¾ teaspoon salt	1 small can pimientos,
2 tablespoons butter	drained, diced fine
1 tablespoon olive oil	1 teaspoon tomato purée or
6 blanched almonds	catsup
2 strips bacon, diced	¼ cup amontillado sherry
1 medium onion, minced	1 cup chicken stock

Make chicken stock by cooking neck, giblets, and wing tips in 2 cups salted, herb-flavored water until liquid is reduced to 1 cup. Strain liquid. Meantime, dust chicken with salt, brown on all sides in butter and oil; remove from pan. Add blanched almonds, brown lightly; remove. Add bacon, onion, garlic, and pimiento and cook until onion is soft. Add remaining ingredients and place chicken in sauce. Simmer uncovered until chicken is tender, about 15 minutes. Top with browned almonds to serve. Makes 4 servings.

POLLO TROPICAL (Chicken Tropical Style)

1 3-pound chicken, cut up, or	1 cup grapes, halved and
2 smaller chickens, quartered	seeded
1 teaspoon salt	⅛ teaspoon powdered cumin
1 tablespoon flour	½ cup dry white wine
3 tablespoons butter	2 tablespoons brandy
1 small white onion, minced	

Dust chicken pieces with salt and flour. Brown chicken in butter over high heat until crisply brown. Remove chicken, add onion and grapes to pan, stir over moderate heat until lightly browned. Add cumin, wine, and brandy, bring to a boil, and boil until reduced about ⅓. Transfer chicken to casserole, add wine-grape mixture, cover casserole, and bake in preheated oven at 375° for 30 minutes. Serves 3 or 4 persons.

It was at the Palace Hotel in Madrid that we first had duck with oranges, and because this was an internationally famous hotel, I assumed that we were dining on what is essentially a French dish. Later it was pointed out to me that the dish originated in Spain, and that the French learned the dish from the Spanish—it may have been one of the Spanish specialties which Maria Theresa took to the French court when she became the bride of Louis XIV in 1660. The oranges used are the bitter oranges of Seville; the peel is what gives the sauce its luscious flavor. Tiny, paper-thin strips of the peel floated in the sauce, give it attractive color as well as spicy flavor.

PATO CON NARANJAS (Duck with Oranges)

2 ducklings, 4 to 5 pounds each	1 tiny garlic clove, crushed
Salt	1 tablespoon butter
Juice ½ lemon	1 cup white wine
2 large oranges	1 tablespoon flour
2 slices onion	1½ cups stock
	Water cress

Because the ducklings in our markets are so fat, they should either be roasted on a rack in the oven or in a rotisserie—I much prefer the latter. Rub with salt and lemon juice before impaling on rotisserie spit or putting on rack, and fill cavity with a sprig of water cress. Roast slowly at 325° in oven or over moderate fire of charcoal (follow manufacturer's directions if using a rotisserie). Meantime, peel one of the oranges very carefully with a sharp knife, so that none of white mem-

brane is cut away. Cut this peel in thin slivers. Cut away the
thin membrane around orange, slice the orange as thin as
possible, put aside for garnish. Squeeze the other orange, saving the juice. Sauté the onion, garlic, and the thin slivers of
orange peel in butter over low heat until onion is soft. Set
aside. Pour off fat from pan as duck roasts (even when spit-
roasted over charcoal, it is important to have a pan under duck
and to remove fat from time to time). Save this, pouring it in
a bowl or jar and place in freezer or freezing compartment of
refrigerator to cause fat to come to top (half an hour); save
what little stock is at bottom. Baste duck with some of orange
juice blended with wine as it roasts, catching the drippings.
When leg of duck moves easily, remove from oven or rotisserie
spit, placing in warm place. Spoon off all fat from drippings.
Add flour to dripping pan or roasting pan, cook over low heat
until it browns, then add the onion-orange-peel mixture and
the fat-free drippings plus remaining orange juice and wine. If
this does not make 1½ cups, add water as needed. Simmer
over moderate heat until well blended, stirring frequently. Add
salt as needed. One duckling serves 2 or 3 persons; for a dinner
party of 6, you will need 2 ducklings. Serve duck garnished
with orange slices and water cress. Brown-crusted potatoes and
asparagus or broccoli are perfect as accompaniments.

PATO A LA SEVILLANA (Duck with Olives)

2 ducklings, 4 to 5 pounds each	¼ cup amontillado sherry
¼ cup salted flour	½ bay leaf, crushed
¼ cup olive oil	1 teaspoon minced parsley
2 garlic cloves, peeled	Pinch of rosemary
2 medium onions, sliced	2 oranges, peeled, sliced
1 medium can (1 pound) tomatoes	1 cup chicken broth
	12 large pimiento-stuffed olives

This is best for wild duck, but domestic Long Island ducklings can be used if cooked the day before and the duck chilled

so that all the fat can rise to the top and be skimmed off. Have ducks cut into quarters; dust each quarter with salted flour, then brown in the hot olive oil with a slice or two of onion in the oil to prevent spattering. At the same time, place the peeled garlic cloves in the oil until well browned, then remove and discard. When duck is browned, remove to a casserole. Pour off excess fat, leaving only ¼ cup in pan. Add onions to oil, cook slowly until tender, then add strained tomatoes, sherry, herbs, and one of the oranges peeled and sliced. Simmer sauce uncovered about 30 minutes, add chicken broth and replace duck, cook uncovered over very low heat until duck is fork-tender; if it is wild duck and young, about 40 minutes. If domestic duck, cook 30 minutes, turn off heat, and when cool enough place in refrigerator. Leave 12 to 24 hours, skim off all fat and reheat duck, cooking until tender. Serve duck in the sauce garnished with sliced olives and the second orange, thinly sliced. Serves 4 to 6 persons.

* * *

Philip II, or Felipe Segundo in the Spanish, is considered by the Spanish people as their greatest king—because during his reign Spain reached its zenith as an empire. Portraits of Felipe Segundo are to be seen everywhere, and El Escorial, the monastery which Philip had built on a hillside not far from Madrid, remains as a monument to him, preserved tenderly by the Spanish Government. This, the guide told us, is the largest building in the world—next to the American Pentagon! Philip was a deeply religious man, a severe, rather dour type, to judge from his portraits, who spent many hours every day on his knees in his private chapel. El Escorial is probably the most ornate monastery ever constructed, so beautiful, in fact, that later monarchs used it as a palace. Much has been made of the fact that the tiny room in which Philip died was bare of ornament, sparsely furnished, almost a hermit's room. However, the day we visited El Escorial the enormous monastery-palace was bitterly cold—as it must have been during the winters when Philip himself lived here, and Philip's bedroom, plain as it was, was located on the sunny side of the mountain, with a magnificent view of the valley spreading below, almost the only room we entered which was at all warm.

Philip had four wives, only one of whom he loved. She was a French princess, his third wife, who bore him two daughters, to whom he was truly devoted: he wrote tender letters to them in his old age. A son was born to his first wife, and Philip is said to have remarked of this puny, not very bright child, "God gave me everything—except a son." (This prince, Don Carlos, died mysteriously, and historic gossip implies that it may not have been by accident. The prince was prone to doing things like running naked in the snow and looking blankly at those who questioned him.) The defeat of the Spanish Armada was also interpreted by Philip as an act of God, since an unexpected Atlantic gale dashed the ships to the Irish rocks.

There is nothing to indicate that Philip inherited the gluttonous interest in food which drove his father, Charles V, to an early grave. Yet he must have had skilled cooks in the royal kitchens, for the following recipe for partridge, named for Philip, is truly a gustatory delight. I tried it once, extravagantly, with lovely plump partridges. However, since partridges are so expensive—when they can be found in our markets—I tried it the second time with whole chicken breasts, and this, I can attest, is elegant enough for the most important company.

PERDIZ FELIPE SEGUNDO
(Partridges—or Chicken Breasts—in the style of Philip II)

4 partridges or whole chicken breasts
¼ cup chopped cooked ham
¼ cup minced, garlic-flavored sausage
1 tablespoon minced white onion

1 cup soft bread crumbs
¼ teaspoon salt
¼ cup olive oil
1 teaspoon paprika
1 teaspoon salt
½ cup orange juice
1 cup seedless white grapes

Combine ham, sausage, onion, bread crumbs, and ¼ teaspoon salt. Use as stuffing for partridge or chicken breasts, tying the breasts with string to hold together during baking. Brush outside of breasts with oil, which has been blended with paprika and 1 teaspoon salt. Place in shallow casserole. Place stemmed whole grapes around birds or chicken. Bake in preheated oven at 350° until delicately browned, about 35 minutes. Brush with oil and baste with orange juice once or twice. Remove birds and grapes to platter, placing over a mound of cooked rice. With drippings left in pan, make a thin sauce: blend a teaspoon of cornstarch with 1 cup water, add to pan, place over moderate heat, stirring until all browned bits are absorbed and sauce is translucent. Serve sauce separately. Serves 4.

PERDIZ A LA MESONERA (Partridges Innkeeper Style)

4 rock Cornish hens, squabs, or partridges
¼ cup olive oil
1 teaspoon paprika
½ teaspoon salt
2 medium onions, minced
1 carrot, grated
1 stalk celery, minced
¼ cup minced cooked ham
½ cup dry white wine
1 cup chicken broth

Rub trussed birds all over with a mixture of the oil, paprika, and salt. Place a few celery leaves inside each bird. Pour remaining oil over bottom of deep casserole, arrange minced vegetables and ham over the oil, place birds on the vegetables. Bake uncovered in preheated oven at 400° for 15 minutes, lower heat to 275°, bake 45 minutes longer, basting occasionally with wine and broth (broth may be made with bouillon cube or powdered chicken-broth concentrate and water). When birds are roasted, transfer to warmed plates, 1 to a serving. Make a sauce with vegetables and broth remaining in casserole, adding water for desired consistency; transfer to saucepan, simmer 4 or 5 minutes. Serves 4.

PERDIZ SOBRE CANAPE (Flamed Partridges)

Brush 4 partridges (or rock Cornish game hens or tiny broiler chickens) with olive oil or a combination of olive oil and melted butter. Place a piece of lean ham or Canadian bacon on the inside of each, or a peeled small onion. Arrange partridges in baking pan, place in preheated oven at 400°, bake until nicely browned, brushing occasionally with oloroso or cream sherry. (Baking time depends on size of bird: test legs; when they move easily, bird is tender.)

Meantime, sauté livers of the birds in butter with a few scrapings of onion. When tender, mash to a paste, spread over 4 slices of white toast, crusts removed. When birds are tender, place one on each slice of bread. Flame with brandy by warming it in small skillet or saucepan, set aflame, pour flaming over birds. Serve with golden-crusted potatoes and water cress. Serves 4 persons.

CHAPTER 9

Legumbres y Ensaladas

(VEGETABLES AND SALADS)

The vegetable in Spain has a role different from that of ours. Either it is served solo as a first course (or an entree), dressed up, of course, with sauce or fancy seasonings, or it becomes an ingredient in a casserole or stew. In most restaurants, if you want a green vegetable along with your meat course, you must order it separately. This does not mean the Spanish skimp on vegetables—week in, week out, they probably consume far more than we do, for vegetables appear on Spanish tables as dinner or supper entrees quite frequently.

(There are exceptions, of course: in some of the big hotels and restaurants, not just one but three or four vegetables may be served with the meat course, and this often is true in wealthier homes, too. In most cases, however, vegetables seem to be judged on their own merits rather than as "background music.")

Oddly, salads are not often listed on restaurant menus. Yet this is the land where the saying originated, "It takes four men to make a salad: a spendthrift for oil, a miser for vinegar, a counselor for salt, and a madman to mix them all up." Salad is, however, always available for the asking, and in Spain invariably it means greens with a simple oil-and-vinegar dressing, tossed at table, as salads should always be prepared. Fancy arranged salads and gelatin molds are considered *entremeses* (hors d'oeuvres) and are more likely to appear on the buffet for a cold lunch or supper.

As my friend Ann Tuttle has made clear, there is rarely much selection of vegetables in the Spanish markets; the Spanish cook is limited to whatever is in season. There will be a deluge of peas and asparagus, for example, for a month or two, then none at all of these two, except in cans, for another year. Instead, there will be little else but green beans and squash. However, the Spanish canned peas are better than ours, more flavorful, greener. Why this should be I cannot explain. Tomatoes are always available, fresh tomatoes with real tomato flavor, and for me this made up for many other lacks.

Asparagus originated in Spain. Back in Roman days, Roman gourmets imported it from Hispania, as they called the land. The Spanish today grow both green and white asparagus, which is used in many diverse ways. In the early spring, wild asparagus is considered a delicacy, slightly bitter though it is. Most popular dressing for asparagus is mayonnaise, freshly made Spanish mayonnaise, fragrant with olive oil.

Very likely the Romans brought the artichoke to Spain, a vegetable beloved throughout the Mediterranean region. Usually one is served only the artichoke hearts, though occasionally it may be the tender artichoke bottoms. These, for *entremeses* topped with a seafood mixture, are quite delicious. We were in Spain during artichoke season, and not once did we see the whole artichokes served, leaves and all. Occasionally, so I was told, the whole artichoke is stuffed, filled with a garlicky ham mixture in the hollow where the choke has been removed, then baked in the oven or poached in a fragrant sauce.

The Moors probably brought the eggplant from the East, and certainly many of the Spanish ways of preparing eggplant reflect the lasting Moorish touch. They also brought almonds, which appear with nearly everything, including vegetables, and they brought rice, and sugar cane, and mint for flavoring. Beans flavored with mint are unique and delicious. Saffron is another Moorish gift—potatoes fried in olive oil, spiced with saffron, topped with almonds make a most wonderful dish.

Yet how the Spanish got along before the conquistadores brought home the tomato and the pimiento in the sixteenth century is hard to imagine. The Spanish tomato sauce, made with pimiento, onion, garlic, and olive oil, goes into virtually everything from soup to—and including—nuts. (Or, to be more literal, nuts go into tomato sauce!)

In Spain, as in all the Mediterranean countries, cooked vegetables are often served cold with an olive oil dressing. In summer, especially, these are delectable. For that matter, I frequently serve vegetables marinated in an oil-and-vinegar dressing for buffet suppers in winter, instead of tossed green salad. A salad must be mixed at the last moment; marinated vegetables not only can be prepared a day ahead, they improve with flavor upon standing.

ALCACHOFAS (Artichokes)

Artichokes and olive oil go together like love and marriage. To cook fresh artichokes, add olive oil to the water in which they are to cook, along with salt (about 2 tablespoons of oil to 2 cups water). Simmer gently until tender, usually about 30 minutes, then drain on rack upside down. I like them whole, pulling the leaves off one by one and dipping them in a vinaigrette dressing. The artichoke bottoms we often save for a second meal, however, trimming them neatly, topping them with a seafood mixture or tuna or ham salad, to serve as hors d'oeuvres. Keep the bottoms marinated in vinaigrette sauce, covered, in the refrigerator until ready to serve again.

Frozen Artichoke Hearts. Place the frozen block in a heavy saucepan with ¼ cup olive oil, ⅛ teaspoon salt, 1 small peeled garlic clove (whole), and ½ teaspoon instant minced onion or grated onion juice. Cover, bring to a boil, lower heat, cook until tender, about 7 minutes, stirring once or twice to break up frozen block. *Add no water.* Remove garlic clove before serving. Sprinkle with lemon juice or vinegar. Delicious both hot and cold. (Instead of onion and garlic a pinch of orégano may be added for seasoning if preferred.)

ALCACHOFAS SALTEADAS (Artichokes with Ham)

Cook frozen artichoke hearts as above, but add ¼ cup minced ham. Omit garlic if you prefer.

ALCACHOFAS A LA GRANADINA
(Artichokes Granada Style)

1 *small onion, sliced*	½ *teaspoon salt*
1 *carrot, finely diced or grated*	Dash *of pepper*
4 *tablespoons olive oil*	1 *cup chicken broth*
1 *package frozen artichoke*	½ *teaspoon rosemary*
hearts	½ *teaspoon lemon juice*

Cook onion and carrot in olive oil over moderate heat until tender. Place artichoke hearts over the onion and carrot, sprinkle with salt and pepper. Cover, cook 2 or 3 minutes, break up frozen block. Add chicken broth and rosemary, cover again, cook until artichokes are tender, about 4 minutes longer. Add lemon juice. Serve artichokes in the unthickened sauce; or, if a thickened sauce is preferred, add 1 teaspoon cornstarch, simmer until smooth and thickened. Serves 3 or 4 persons.

BERENJENAS (Eggplant)

Like the artichoke, the eggplant needs olive oil, and I personally cannot imagine using any other fat or oil in the cooking of it. Eggplant takes on a surprisingly "meaty" flavor when cooked in olive oil. In fact, when it is in the height of season and the vegetable fully ripe when picked, it can be diced and simmered in olive oil, needing no seasoning other than a sprinkling of salt and pepper, perhaps a dash of onion salt. Like so many of our supermarket vegetables, however, eggplants when shipped from long distances have already lost much flavor and consequently must be cooked longer, with other flavorings added to make up for their lack of freshness.

The peel of the eggplant (especially when it is garden-fresh) has more flavor than the pulp, and, when gently cooked in olive oil, will be tender and delicious. Its shiny blackness makes the vegetable more attractive in appearance, too. I have always been told that eggplant should be soaked first in salt water, that doing this will prevent its absorbing so much oil in cooking. However, I am not convinced that this is true. I have tried both ways, and find the salt-water soaking quite unnecessary. Eggplant, cooked the Mediterranean way, is one of my favorite vegetables. I like it even better cold than hot, especially in warm weather, a flavorful entree for lunch, a marvelous late-evening snack, especially when accompanied by dry sherry or beer. (These two beverages, incidentally, are much alike in flavor—and both complement the rich heartiness of eggplant deliciously.)

BERENJENAS A LA ESPANOLA (Eggplant Spanish Style)

1 small eggplant or ½ large
eggplant, unpeeled, diced
⅓ cup olive oil
1 medium onion, minced
1 or 2 garlic cloves, crushed

¼ teaspoon salt
1 teaspoon minced parsley
3 tablespoons tomato sauce or
1 large tomato, peeled,
chopped

Combine all ingredients, simmer slowly in a heavy iron skillet until tender, about 30 minutes, stirring once or twice. In summer, wrap in a double thickness of aluminum foil, place in coals of barbecue grill, cook about 1 hour, shifting the foil package once or twice. Makes 4 delicious servings.

BERENJENAS SENORITO (Baked Eggplant Young Master)

4 small eggplants (4 inches
long)
6 medium tomatoes or 1 large
(1 pound 12 ounces) can
1 onion, minced
⅓ cup olive oil

½ pound (1 cup) diced
cooked ham
Salt and pepper to taste
1 teaspoon garlic powder
4 slices bread, crumbled
4 eggs, poached or fried
4 rolled anchovy fillets

Cut a horizontal slice from the side of each eggplant; scoop out center, leaving shell ¼ inch thick. Dice scooped-out pulp, discarding seedier portions. Peel and chop tomatoes; sauté with onion in olive oil until soft. Add ham, salt and pepper, garlic powder, and eggplant pulp. Cook until eggplant is tender. Add bread crumbs. Brush eggplant shells inside and out with olive oil, stuff with mixture. Place in oiled pan or wide, shallow casserole. Bake uncovered in a preheated 400° oven for 20 to 25 minutes. During last 5 minutes gently fry or poach the eggs; place one egg on each stuffed eggplant. In center of egg, place a rolled anchovy fillet. Makes 4 meal-in-a-dish servings.

BERENJENAS RELLENAS A LA ANDALUZ
(Stuffed Eggplant Andalusian Style)

4 *small eggplants*
½ *cup olive oil*
1 *small onion, chopped*
1 *pimiento, cut in strips*
2 *tablespoons minced ham*

½ *teaspoon salt*
⅛ *teaspoon pepper*
1 *cup soft bread crumbs tossed*
  with 1 tablespoon olive oil

This is best when small eggplants are used, 1 for each serving, though it can be done with one very large eggplant, which then would be sliced into serving portions at table. Cut a horizontal slice off the side of each eggplant, scoop out center, leaving a shell ½ inch thick. Add olive oil to deep heavy pan, add eggplant, simmer gently, covered, 10 minutes. Remove carefully so as to keep shells intact. Meantime, make stuffing by sautéing onion, pimiento, and ham in 2 tablespoons olive oil until onion is tender; add eggplant pulp (seeds removed), cook until tender. Season with salt and pepper. Stuff eggplant shells with this mixture, top with the breadcrumbs moistened with oil. Place in preheated 350° oven for 15 minutes or until crumbs are golden.

Serves 4.

BERENJENAS CASERTA (Eggplant Casserole)

1 *medium eggplant (1½*
  pounds)
½ *cup olive oil*
½ *cup fine dry crumbs*
1 *large tomato, peeled and*
  chopped, or 2 tablespoons
  tomato catsup

1 *tablespoon grated Parmesan*
  cheese
1 *or 2 garlic cloves, minced*
1 *tablespoon minced parsley*
1 *tablespoon vinegar*
1 *2-ounce tin anchovy fillets,*
  or 2 tablespoons chopped
  cooked bacon

Cut unpeeled eggplant in thin slices, soak in salt water ½ hour. Dry on towel. Sauté in oil until lightly browned; drain slices on paper towel. Combine remaining ingredients (if anchovies are used, rinse under warm water, then chop fine). Arrange crumb mixture and eggplant slices in layers in 2½-quart casserole. Arrange a layer of additional crumbs on top, tossing crumbs with oil to moisten. Bake uncovered at 350° for 1 hour. Makes 5 or 6 entree servings.

CALABAZA A LA ESPANOLA (Squash Spanish Style)

1½ pounds yellow summer squash
2 medium onions, chopped
½ green pepper, chopped
Black pepper
1½ tablespoons minced fresh tarragon
⅓ cup olive oil
1 teaspoon salt

Dice unpeeled squash into ½-inch pieces, combine with remaining ingredients, cook over moderate heat in heavy skillet or covered saucepan until tender, about 15 minutes. Or, in summer, place in center of large sheet of aluminum foil, place beside coals in bed of barbecue grill and bake, turning foil package occasionally, for at least half an hour. Makes 4 servings.

Note: Zucchini can be cooked the same way, but slice thickly rather than dice.

CALABACINES RELLENOS (Stuffed Baby Squash)

6 small summer squash or zucchini
1 medium onion, minced
1 garlic clove, minced
2 large tomatoes, peeled, chopped
2 tablespoons olive oil
½ teaspoon salt or to taste
Pinch of sugar
2 tablespoons flour
2 tablespoons butter
¼ teaspoon salt
1 cup milk
1 egg, beaten
2 tablespoons grated Gruyère cheese

Cut squash in half lengthwise; scoop out pulp, leaving ½-inch shells. Cook the shells in salted water for 5 minutes; remove carefully to avoid breaking. Cook the scooped-out center (seeds removed), the onion, garlic, and tomatoes in the olive oil until tender; season with salt, sugar, and a dash of pepper, if desired. Stuff the squash shells with this mixture. Arrange stuffed squash in a large shallow baking dish which has been rubbed with oil. Meantime, make a white sauce with the flour, butter, salt, and milk, cooking over low heat until thickened and smooth. Add the egg, blend until smooth, beating quickly to avoid curdling. Pour the sauce over the stuffed squash, top with cheese. To complete cooking, place, uncovered, in preheated 350° oven for 20 minutes or until top is golden. Serves 6 persons.

JUDIAS VERDES A LA ESPANOLA
(Green Beans Spanish Style)

1 pound green beans, or 1 package frozen cut beans	2 pimientos or sweet red peppers, cut in strips
2 tablespoons olive oil	1 tablespoon minced parsley
1 or 2 garlic cloves	Salt and pepper

Cook beans, cut in 1-inch pieces, in salted water about 5 minutes (frozen beans need no precooking). Drain. Heat garlic in olive oil until brown, remove and discard. Add pimientos to oil, brown slightly. Add parsley and a sprinkling of salt and pepper. Add beans, cover, cook until tender over low heat. Makes 4 servings.

* * *

The Spanish *habas* are quite different in flavor from our Lima beans, but since we do not have *habas* in our market, the same recipes can be used for Limas. In fact, I like the Limas far better!

HABAS A LA MONTANESA (Beans Mountain Style)

2 *pounds fresh Limas, shelled,*   3 *fresh tomatoes, peeled and*
   or 1 package frozen Ford-   *diced, or 1-pound can toma-*
   hook Limas   *toes*
¼ *cup olive oil*   1 *tablespoon minced parsley*
2 *slices bacon, diced, or* ¼   ¼ *teaspoon dried mint*
   cup chopped cooked ham   ¼ *teaspoon salt*
2 *tablespoons minced onion*

Combine ingredients (add no water), cook over low heat, covered, in heavy saucepan for 30 minutes for fresh Limas, 15 to 20 minutes for frozen Limas. (Do not defrost beans before adding to pan, but watch carefully, breaking up frozen block after 2 or 3 minutes.) Makes 4 servings.

* * *

Peas are used a great deal in Spain, both as an ingredient in other dishes—omelets, casseroles, and rice dishes—and as a vegetable served plain. Occasionally they are cooked with ham, *salteadas*, as are the artichokes and beans. This is one vegetable I feel is not embellished with olive oil, except, as in the following recipe, when olive oil and butter are used together.

GUISANTES A LA VASCA (Peas Basque Style)

2 *pounds fresh green peas, or*   4 *to 6 small new potatoes,*
   1 *package frozen peas*   *cooked*
2 *tablespoons minced onion*   *Salt and pepper*
1 *tablespoon olive oil*   *Minced parsley*
1 *tablespoon butter*

Cook peas in boiling salted water until barely tender. Separately cook potatoes. Sauté onion in olive oil and butter, add potatoes, sauté until lightly browned, add shelled peas, sprinkle with a little salt and pepper, cover, cook 5 minutes. Add a little minced parsley just before serving. Serves 4.

PATATAS A LA CASTELLANA (Potatoes Castilian Style)

4 medium potatoes, peeled,   ¼ teaspoon saffron
   sliced paper thin   ½ teaspoon salt
4 medium onions, thinly sliced   ¼ cup coarsely chopped al-
1 pimiento, cut in thin strips   monds
¼ cup olive oil

Cook the potatoes, onions, and pimiento in the olive oil
over moderate heat, sprinkling with salt and saffron. (If leaf
saffron is used, soak in 1 tablespoon hot water, add this to
potatoes after they have browned.) Cover tightly; stir once
or twice to prevent sticking. During last 5 minutes add
chopped almonds. Requires approximately 20 minutes. Excellent with hamburgers or *albóndigas* (meat balls) (see
Index).

Makes 6 average servings.

GARBANZOS A LA SEVILLANA (Chick-Peas Seville Style)

1 can (1 pound) chick-peas,   ¼ cup rice
   drained   1 sweet potato
1 small onion, sliced   1 cup water
1 or 2 garlic cloves, minced   ½ teaspoon salt
2 tablespoons olive oil   1 teaspoon minced parsley
1 cup canned tomatoes

Sauté onion and garlic in olive oil until soft, add tomatoes,
drained chick-peas, rice, and sweet potato peeled and cut into
1-inch cubes. Add water and salt, cover, cook 20 minutes or
until potatoes are tender. Add parsley a minute before removing from stove. Astonishingly good! A nice luncheon or supper dish for a meatless meal.

Makes 4 to 6 servings.

GARBANZOS CON JAMON (Chick-Peas with Ham)

*1 can (1 pound) chick-peas,
drained
1 small onion, sliced
2 or 3 tablespoons olive oil*

*1 or 2 garlic cloves, crushed
¼ cup chopped cooked ham
1 tablespoon minced fresh
parsley*

Sauté onion and garlic in the olive oil until soft, add the drained chick-peas and the ham, cook until heated through. Add the parsley. (Or ham may be omitted and the above dish may be served as a vegetable with baked ham, cold or hot.) Makes 3 or 4 servings.

PIMIENTOS RELLENOS (Stuffed Peppers)

*6 large green or red sweet pep-
pers
2 cups cooked rice
Olive oil
1 cup diced leftover chicken,
meat, or fish
6 chopped green olives
1 teaspoon capers
Salt and pepper*

*Soft bread crumbs moistened
with oil
1 can (8 ounces) tomato sauce
2 tablespoons olive oil
1 tablespoon instant minced
onion
1 tablespoon minced parsley
1 bay leaf*

In Spain the peppers are roasted over coals until the outer skin is blistered, then this is peeled off. The reason for doing this is that the outer skin contains most of the bitterness. However, I am satisfied with the results when I simply brush the peppers with oil inside and out before adding the stuffing. Combine the rice, leftover chicken, meat, or fish, the chopped olives, capers, and salt and pepper to taste. Fill the peppers with this mixture, top with the crumbs moistened with oil, and place in a well-oiled baking dish. Brush additional oil over the outside of the peppers after stuffing. Place uncovered in a preheated 350° oven for 15 minutes. Meantime, combine the canned sauce, 2 tablespoons olive oil, instant onion, parsley, and bay leaf and simmer until well blended. Pour the sauce over and around the peppers, bake half an hour longer. Serves 6.

COLIFLOR A LA VINAGRETA (Cauliflower Vinaigrette)

Cook the flowerets of cauliflower until just tender (no more than 5 minutes) in boiling salted water. Drain. Cover with the following sauce.

¼ cup olive oil	Pinch of cayenne pepper
2 tablespoons vinegar	1 hard-cooked egg, chopped
¼ teaspoon salt	1 tablespoon capers
1 tablespoon minced green pepper	

Combine ingredients, pour over hot cauliflower. Serve at once, or let marinate in the sauce several hours to serve cold. One *small* head of cauliflower makes 6 servings.

COLIFLOR FRITO (Fried Cauliflower)

Cut cauliflower into individual flowerets, marinate at least 30 minutes in a mixture of 1 tablespoon vinegar, ¼ cup ice water, 1 slice of onion, and ½ teaspoon salt. Drain well. Dip each floweret in beaten egg then in fine dry crumbs (or in a thick egg batter). Fry in hot olive oil until crisply browned on all sides.

* * *

There are two vegetable stews in Spain, one called *menestra* (probably a word from the Romans, the same root as for *minestrone*), the other called *pisto*. I suspect that the chief difference is one of geography, for in southwestern Spain, when I inquired about pisto, no one seemed to be aware of its existence, yet this is said to be a favorite dish of Castile. Pisto is made in so many different ways it apparently can be almost anything. "Hash" is the closest approximation. Often eggs are added to the mixed cooked vegetables, much as the Basques make their *piperade*. I am so fond of pisto myself I am including three different recipes. The first of these is very much like the dish of Provençal in France called *ratatouille*, and similar to the *caponata* of Italy. Greece, too, has an eggplant dish much like this. In none of the other Mediterranean countries are eggs added to the vegetable hash, however, which apparently is what makes the Spanish pisto unique.

PISTO (1)

¼ cup diced lean ham
¼ cup olive oil
2 large onions, sliced
1 red pepper, seeded and diced, or 2 pimientos, drained, diced

1 small eggplant (or ½ medium), diced, not peeled
2 garlic cloves, minced
1 package frozen artichoke hearts
1 teaspoon salt, or to taste
1 can (1 pound) tomatoes

Sauté ham in olive oil; when lightly browned, add onion, red pepper or pimiento, diced unpeeled eggplant, and garlic. Cook over moderate heat until onions are soft but not brown. Add artichoke hearts, salt, and tomato. Cook covered until artichoke hearts are tender and tomato has cooked to mushy consistency. Wonderful both hot and cold. (Especially cold!) Makes about 6 servings.

PISTO (2)

2 medium onions, chopped
2 medium potatoes, peeled, chopped
2 green peppers, diced
⅓ cup olive oil
1 package frozen Limas, cut green beans, or Italian beans

1 teaspoon salt, or to taste
2 cups canned tomatoes
3 well-beaten eggs
1 tablespoon minced parsley
Fried croutons for garnish

Cook chopped onions, potatoes, and green peppers in olive oil over moderate heat until soft but not browned, turning occasionally to prevent sticking. Add beans, salt, and tomatoes. Cook covered about 30 minutes. To well-beaten eggs add a little of the tomato sauce to blend well, then combine with remaining pisto. Cook over reduced heat, stirring constantly, until eggs are cooked and sauce thickened. Serve at once topped with croutons of bread fried in olive oil. Makes 4 to 6 servings. Better hot, but also can be served cold.

PISTO MANCHEGO

This is a favorite way of preparing pisto in La Mancha, south of Madrid, in the dry, treeless plains of New Castile.

¼ pound lean pork	1 pound zucchini or yellow
4 or 5 tablespoons olive oil	squash, sliced
2 or 3 onions, sliced or chopped	1 can (8 ounces) tomato sauce
1 can (4 ounces) pimientos, diced	½ teaspoon salt, or to taste
	6 eggs, lightly scrambled

Dice pork in fine pieces. Sauté lightly in 2 tablespoons olive oil; push to one side of pan. Add onion and pimiento and 2 more tablespoons oil; simmer cver low heat about 20 minutes, not permitting onions to brown. Remove meat, onions, and pimientos. Add squash and more oil if necessary. Cook until tender but still somewhat crisp. Replace meat, onions, and pimientos, add tomato sauce and salt to taste. Simmer another 15 to 20 minutes. Meantime, beat 3 eggs at a time, season, cook separately in an omelet pan or skillet to make a very thin omelet; cut in strips, set aside. Repeat with remaining eggs. Add strips of egg as garnish to pisto. Makes 4 to 6 entree servings.

MENESTRA DE LEGUMBRES (Vegetable Stew of Andalusia)

¼ cup olive oil
1 slice bread, cubed
1 medium onion, chopped
2 or 3 tomatoes, peeled, chopped
1 cup bouillon
2 carrots, finely diced
1 small yellow squash, diced

1 pimiento, chopped
1 package frozen Fordhook Limas
⅛ teaspoon dried mint, crushed
1 teaspoon minced parsley
Salt to taste

Sauté the bread cubes (crust removed) in the olive oil until golden; remove bread from oil. Add onion and tomatoes, cook until onion is tender. Add remaining ingredients, bring to a boil, simmer gently until vegetables are tender. Serve topped with bread croutons. Makes about 6 servings.

ENSALADA DE LEGUMBRES (Cooked Vegetable Salad)

2 or 3 potatoes, peeled, cooked
1 cup green beans, cooked
3 carrots, cooked, quartered
1 package frozen artichoke hearts, cooked
1 or 2 zucchini sliced, cooked
½ cup olive oil

¼ cup vinegar
1 teaspoon salt, or to taste
¼ teaspoon black pepper
1 tablespoon grated onion
¼ cup chopped stuffed olives
2 tablespoons minced parsley
1 tablespoon capers

All vegetables should be cooked separately until tender but still crisp. Drain, cool. Combine olive oil, vinegar, salt, pepper, and grated onion; divide dressing among vegetables, marinating each vegetable separately. Shortly before serving, arrange vegetables attractively on platter, garnishing with parsley sprigs. Combine chopped olives, parsley, and capers and sprinkle over top. Serves 6 to 8.

PIMIENTOS FRITOS (Sautéed Peppers)

Cut green or red sweet peppers in quarters, seed, and cut away membrane carefully. Sauté in olive oil with a few slices of onion and a whole peeled garlic clove until pepper is tender. Discard garlic clove. Sprinkle with salt. Serve as a vegetable with roast pork, veal, or lamb, along with oven-browned potatoes. (Canned pimientos, well drained, can be cooked in the same way.)

ESPINACAS (Spinach)

Spinach is cooked much the same in Spain as we cook it: Steamed in its own water, chopped, seasoned with butter, salt and pepper. Sometimes olive oil is used with butter, but this completely changes the flavor. With a few drops of vinegar or lemon juice added, it is like a hot salad.

One way I like to prepare it as a change is to brown a garlic clove in olive oil, then discard the garlic clove, add about a teaspoon of grated onion, cook this until soft, then add the spinach and a tablespoon or two of red wine. In fact, this can be done to frozen chopped spinach: cut the frozen block with a sharp knife before adding to the pan, add no water at all, steam in the wine until frozen spinach is softened, then cook about 1 minute longer. Sprinkle with lemon juice before serving, but do *not* add the lemon juice until after the spinach has been removed from the pan or the vegetable will turn brown.

Creamed spinach (cooked, puréed, blended with a little heavy cream or cream sauce) is often served topped with croutons, bread cubes fried until crisp in olive oil.

JUDIAS VERDES ESCABECHE (Pickled Green Beans)

Cook whole green beans, the young, tender kind, in boiling salted water until they can be pierced with fork but are still crisp. Marinate at least 1 hour in the following sauce. (Canned green beans can also be dressed this way.)

SAUCE

¾ cup tarragon vinegar
3 tablespoons olive oil
1 crushed garlic clove, or ¼ teaspoon instant minced garlic softened in water

1½ tablespoons sugar
1½ teaspoons salt
½ teaspoon freshly ground black pepper

Arrange bundles of the marinated green beans inside rings of thinly sliced sweet onion, then place on salad greens.

ENSALADA TROPICAL (Tropical Fruit Salad)

4 small bananas, cut lengthwise
2 oranges, cut in sections or diced
1 pimiento or sweet red pepper, cut in strips
¼ cup shredded coconut

SAUCE

¼ cup olive oil
1 teaspoon grated onion
½ teaspoon salt
Dash pepper
¼ teaspoon crushed dried mint or 1 teaspoon minced fresh mint

Arrange fruit and pimiento in bowl, marinate 30 minutes to 1 hour in the dressing. Serve on lettuce sprinkled with coconut. Enough for 4 servings.

ENSALADA DE TOMATES (Tomato Salad)

Sliced ripe tomatoes will keep fresh without weeping for an hour or longer when covered with olive oil. Just before serving, sprinkle with a bit of onion salt (if you like), minced tarragon or parsley, salt and pepper, and a few drops of vinegar. Makes a luscious sauce.

SALSA DE ALMENDRAS (Almond Salad Dressing)

8 blanched almonds
1 or 2 garlic cloves
½ teaspoon salt

1 cup olive oil
¼ cup wine vinegar

Crush almonds and garlic to a paste with mortar and pestle; work in salt. Slowly beat in olive oil, then the vinegar. A good dressing for any green salad.

ENSALADA VALENCIANA (Salad Valencia Style)

This is my favorite salad. We have it in our house about once every week.

2 oranges, peeled thinly sliced	2 tablespoons red wine vinegar
1 small onion, thinly sliced	¼ teaspoon salt
4 tablespoons olive oil	Freshly ground black pepper
	Salad greens

Marinate oranges and onion in olive oil, vinegar, salt and pepper for 15 minutes to one hour. Add to salad greens, toss. For variation, you may add pimiento-stuffed olives or strips of bright red pimiento. Black olives are good with it, too. Makes about 4 servings.

SALSA DE MENTA (Mint Dressing)

Crush 6 or 7 fresh mint leaves with a large clove of garlic in mortar with pestle or in salad bowl, using back of wooden spoon. Add ⅓ cup olive oil, 2 tablespoons lemon juice, and salt and pepper to taste. Excellent with citrus salad.

ENSALADA MIXTA (1) (Mixed Seafood Salad)

1 cooked lobster (1½ pounds) or 2 cooked rock lobster tails	1 medium onion, thinly sliced
½ pound shelled shrimp, cooked	2 tablespoons vinegar
3 chopped hard-cooked eggs	½ teaspoon Dijon mustard
2 gherkin pickles, chopped	4 tablespoons olive oil
1 tablespoon capers	Salt and pepper to taste
	2 pimientos, cut in strips

Remove lobster meat from shell, cut in cubes. Add remaining ingredients, except olive oil and pimiento, toss to blend. Chill. Just before serving, add olive oil, toss lightly. Serve over salad greens garnished with strips of pimiento and, if desired, slices of hard-cooked egg.

ENSALADA MIXTA (2) (Mixed Seafood Salad)

1 can (7 ounces) tuna fish, drained

¼ cup sliced chorizo, cooked, or diced salami

4 ounces ham, cut in thin strips

2 or 3 tomatoes, quartered

1 small onion, thinly sliced

¼ cup olive oil

¼ teaspoon salt

Freshly ground black pepper

1½ tablespoons vinegar

4 hard-cooked eggs, quartered

Chop tuna in big chunks, combine in bowl with sausage, ham, tomatoes, and onion. Cover with olive oil, salt and pepper, and vinegar. Marinate half an hour. Arrange over salad greens with eggs arranged as garnish. Sprinkle a little of the dressing over the eggs to keep them fresh until served. Luncheon salad for 2 to 3 persons.

ENSALADA DE BOQUERON Y ACEITUNA (Olive and Anchovy Salad)

2 anchovy fillets, minced

2 tablespoons minced pimiento

¼ cup olive oil

1½ tablespoons vinegar

½ teaspoon salt

1 cup pitted or stuffed green olives

½ teaspoon dry mustard

Pinch of cumin

About 1 quart salad greens

Combine all ingredients but greens, blend well, let stand several hours before adding to salad greens, which have been washed, crisped in refrigerator, and torn into bite-size pieces. Enough to serve 4 persons.

CHAPTER 10

Postres

(DESSERTS)

The dessert section on a Spanish restaurant menu is small and usually consists almost entirely of fruit served up in various guises. This does not mean that the Spanish are uninterested in sweets—there are pastry shops everywhere, and the pastries tend to be very, very sweet. But sweets are consumed with coffee, tea, or chocolate about six or seven o'clock of the late afternoon, halfway between lunch and dinner. Or they are enjoyed on special occasions such as christenings, feast days, birthdays, or other anniversaries.

Few pastries seem to be made at home—perhaps because not many kitchens in Spain have ovens. I recall one night accompanying a Spanish friend to a convent to pick up some *yemas*, the little lemony confections said to have been created by St. Teresa back in the sixteenth century. In the cloister he rang a small bell and presently the door of a dumb-waiter opened. There on the shelf was a box of the goodies wrapped to be carried away. He placed a few coins on the dumb-waiter in payment, the door closed again automatically, and we walked away without seeing a soul.

Among the sweets for sale in the pastry shops are dozens of tiny *pasteles*, little pastries some of which look a bit like pralines, thin and crisp, studded with nuts, but curled up like a leaf . . . thin rolls of chocolate filled sometimes with marshmallow, sometimes with whipped cream . . . thumb-size little cakes frosted over and garnished with nuts or candied fruit . . . balls rolled in powdered sugar which, when bitten into, revealed a soft, custardy heart.

Bizcocho means cake and so does *tarta*, and I could not figure out any difference between the two. My daughter was always longing for cake, so whenever we saw either a bizcocho or a tarta listed on a restaurant menu, she tried it. Invariably the cake itself was like our spongecake, but dressed up with different fillings and frostings or garnishes.

The national dessert of Spain is *flan*—nothing else in the world but simple caramel custard. Now and then one encounters *flan al ron* or *flan con nata* (whipped cream) or some other variation; once I had it with *cabello de ángel*, a squash-like vegetable of southern Spain which when cooked in syrup breaks into candied threads. *Tortilla al ron*, omelet flamed with rum, is another dessert commonly encountered. If the Spanish don't have omelet in one guise, it seems that they must have it in another, day after day!

Ice cream, naturally, is a favorite dessert in Spain, as it is all over the world, and most often in restaurants it is served in a pastry shell, called *tarta de helado*.

Chocolate is encountered less often than one would expect

in the country which first introduced the cacao bean to Europe. It is consumed everywhere as a beverage, frequently served for breakfast, and occasionally it even appears in sauces for partridge, or veal stew, or even for tongue. I did not encounter any of these dishes while I was in Spain, but I heard about them and once tried in my own kitchen adding chocolate to a beef stew according to a Spanish recipe in a book. It was very good, surprisingly good—not sweet at all. However, it was not a dish I would care to repeat often. I have included one very rich and wonderful chocolate dessert, *Marquesa de Chocolate*, which was served at a luncheon in the Terry home in Puerto de Santa María. Señora de Terry, matriarch of the Spanish-Irish family that owns the fourth-largest sherry bodega in Spain, gave me her own recipe, which I have since served several times at home.

Whether the dessert is an elaborate pastry or simply *fruta del tiempo* (fruit of the season) or *queso* (cheese), invariably it will be followed by Spanish brandy (*coñac*) or a fine oloroso sherry or a tiny glass of anise liqueur. To my mind this is the perfect way to end a good dinner: with a little *digestivo* served in a glass, to sip reflectively over mellow conversation.

Frutas Del Tiempo

NARANJAS (Oranges)

The oranges of Spain are deliciously, wonderfully sweet, and, thanks to modern horticulture, they are available throughout the year. Orange trees in Spain bear several crops during the year, with sometimes both blossom and fruit on the tree at the same time. There are many different varieties of orange trees, the best coming from the Valencia area, on the east coast, and the area south of Seville, in the southwest, where Mairena oranges are grown. The bitter oranges of Seville are

the oldest, very likely were the "golden apples of the Hes-
perides," which, according to Greek mythology, Hercules was
sent to seek. The sweeter oranges are said to have been
brought in later from the Indies, probably by the Moors. Today bitter and sweet varieties are sometimes grafted together
to make a hardier tree, for there are orange trees in Seville
six and seven hundred years old, still bearing fruit.

A fresh orange was my dessert virtually every day we were
in Spain. A whole orange is brought to you on a plate (or you
may choose from a bowl of assorted fruits), along with knife
and fork. Peeling an orange is not difficult when the fruit can
be held firmly in place with the fork, and a sharp knife used
to cut the rind away. Then the peeled fruit is cut up with
knife and fork and eaten daintily, without being touched once
by fingers. Americans make so much fuss about nutrition, vita-
mins, well-balanced diets, and so on, yet somehow this wonderful European custom of serving fresh fruit as dessert has
never caught on with us. I wonder why? In American restaurants again and again I beg for a single orange (or a single apple) for dessert, *au naturel*—and there never seems to be a
single one available in the entire establishment.

I'd like to start a campaign for a fruit bowl in every American restaurant. Anyone care to join me?

Meantime, for those who prefer their oranges already cut
up, here are some serving suggestions.

NARANJAS AL VINO TINTO (Oranges in Red Wine)

Peel and slice or dice oranges, sprinkle lightly with sugar,
cover with red wine. Marinate an hour or longer.

NARANJAS AL CONAC (Brandied Oranges)

Peel and dice 4 to 6 navel oranges, place in bowl, add ¼
cup Spanish brandy, 2 tablespoons honey, and a pinch of cinnamon. Blend well, let stand several hours until time to serve.

MELOCOTONES EN ALMIBAR (Peaches in Syrup)

When a Spanish restaurant menu lists this item, you will find it means simply peaches out of a can. Fresh peaches, simmered gently in brandy-flavored syrup, are something else again.

10 to 12 ripe peaches	1 cup water
1 cup sugar	¼ to ½ cup brandy

Peel peaches, leaving them whole. (Or, if you prefer, cut them in half, but place stones in the syrup for flavor.) Heat sugar and water in roomy kettle until sugar is dissolved but not boiling; add whole peaches, simmer 15 minutes. Add brandy, let cool. Transfer to smaller bowl, keep in refrigerator until serving time. Pass heavy cream at table. Makes 6 to 8 servings.

MELOCOTONES CON HELADO (Peaches with Ice Cream)

This is a simple peach sundae, using canned peaches, but a dash of brandy, oloroso sherry, or gold rum gives the peach syrup more luscious flavor.

COMPOTA DE MELOCOTON (Peaches Compote)

6 to 8 fresh peaches, peeled	1 or 2 oranges, peeled and
2 tablespoons sugar	diced
	1 tablespoon curaçao or rum

Combine sliced peaches and oranges, add sugar and curaçao or rum, let stand in refrigerator several hours. Makes 6 servings.

MELOCOTONES CON VINO BLANCO
(Peaches in White Wine)

Peel and slice fresh peaches, add sugar to taste, then cover with dry white wine and add a sprinkling of anise liqueur or Pernod. Chill thoroughly before serving.

PERAS (Pears)

Ripe sweet pears, like oranges, are most often served whole, with knife and fork. Canned pears *en almíbar* also make a delicious dessert when some of the syrup is poured off, replaced with a little gold rum (to taste) and a touch of curaçao.

HIGOS (Figs)

There are fig trees all over the southern part of Spain, and some of them bear two kinds of fruit on the same tree, first a white fig, then a black fig—and both luscious. The Moors also brought the fig to Spain, and the way of preparing them is an Arabic heritage. The fig trees were just beginning to blossom when we were in Málaga, a city with a breath-taking view of the Mediterranean. The ancient fortress which towers high over the city, the Gibralfaro (meaning in Arabic "Hill of the Watchtower"), originally was an Iberian stronghold, then the Moors occupied a fortress on the ancient foundations, planting exquisite gardens—including many fig trees, inside the turreted walls. Climbing over the ruins today, one can peek through the slits of windows in the turrets and wander in the tiny chambers where prisoners were held, seeing the hooks to which their chains were fastened still imbedded in the stone. From these towers, the walls descend sharply to the sea. No doubt the poor devils confined in those tiny cells had little thought for the beauty of the sea or of the Moorish gardens but to us, viewing it all as tourists, it was captivating and romantic. A tunnel led from the Gibralfaro direct to the

Alcazaba below, the palace where the caliphs lived sumptuously with gardens on successive levels, each blossoming with peach, almond, pear, orange, and fig trees in addition to flowers of every description. Perfume urns still stand in each room of this palace of the Moors, so that the air could be made fragrant before each meal.

A restaurant is now located on the brow of the Gibralfaro, a place worth visiting for its view as much as its food. The following way of preparing figs is a specialty of the house. For Americans living in California or other areas where fig trees grow, ripe figs may be prepared this way, or canned figs may be used any time of the year, wherever you live.

HIGOS CON VINO MALAGUENO
(Fresh Figs in Málaga Wine)

10 to 12 ripe figs
¼ cup confectioners' sugar
½ teaspoon cinnamon
2 tablespoons brandy

2 tablespoons Málaga wine
(or muscatel or a cream
sherry may be used)

Place figs in layers in a bowl, dust with sugar and cinnamon, then sprinkle with the brandy and let stand 1 to 2 hours. Add wine, toss to blend flavors. Serve with a little heavy cream or ice cream. Makes 3 or 4 servings.

HIGOS EN ALMIBAR CON HELADO
(Figs in Syrup with Ice Cream)

To a large can of figs in heavy syrup, add a tablespoon of Málaga wine or 1 of curaçao (I prefer the latter). Let stand an hour or so, then drain syrup, boil until reduced to a thick syrup. Place 2 figs on each serving of ice cream, add 1 or 2 tablespoons of syrup, garnish with toasted almonds.

GRANADAS (Pomegranates)

Pomegranates grow in profusion throughout southern Spain. "*Granada*" comes from the Latin "*pomegranatum,*" meaning "apple of many seeds." Very likely the trees were brought from the Orient hundreds of years before the caliphs of Granada enjoyed the pomegranate syrup chilled into an icy sherbet. Pomegranate syrup may be found in gourmet shops in our own country. It makes a luscious topping for ice cream.

Otherwise, for those who like to nibble long at fruit the many-seeded apple makes a lovely dessert, with Spanish brandy or a smooth brown cream sherry.

FRESAS (Strawberries)

Strawberries in Spain are wonderfully sweet, especially the tiny *fresas* (the larger variety are called *fresones*), which often are brought to the table with the caps still on, served on a doily of bright green leaves. Here are some other delicious ways of serving them.

With brandy. Sprinkle berries with sugar and a little brandy, let stand an hour or more until ready to serve.

In orange juice. Sprinkle berries with sugar, cover with ½ cup orange juice, top with shredded coconut.

With red wine. Marinate sugared berries in red wine, at room temperature, at least half an hour, or up to 24 hours.

PINA AL KIRSCH (Pineapple with Kirsch)

When you see pineapple listed on a Spanish menu, it usually means canned pineapple, probably imported from the United States. Occasionally fresh pineapple is available, from the Canary Islands or North Africa. Both canned and fresh pineapple slices are always improved with a sprinkling of kirschwasser, the Swiss cherry liqueur.

PLATANOS (Small Bananas)

A bowl of *fruta del tiempo* invariably includes tiny bananas from the Canary Islands. These are not as good as ours, at least not when eaten from the skin, though when fried or caramelized in syrup they can be delicious. Flamed with rum, a heritage from the old Spanish colonies in the Caribbean, they make a luscious dessert.

PLATANOS AL RON (Bananas in Rum Sauce)

8 *small bananas, cut in half lengthwise*	*Pinch of powdered cloves*
1 *cup brown sugar*	*Pinch of powdered ginger*
½ *teaspoon cinnamon*	8 *tablespoons butter*
	1 *small can crushed pineapple*
	¼ *cup dark sweet rum, heated*

Roll bananas in the sugar, which has been blended with the spices. Sauté in butter until lightly browned and sugar begins to caramelize. Place in layers in a shallow casserole or decorative skillet that can be brought to table, sprinkling more of the sugar-spice mixture over each layer, but saving out 2 tablespoons. Pour the crushed pineapple with its syrup over the bananas, add the reserved sugar mixture. Place in oven preheated to 350° until top begins to caramelize. Remove from oven, spoon heated rum over top, lighting rum. Carry flaming to table. This is very sweet but quite delicious. Serves 4 generously.

MELON

There are many wonderful melons in Spain, sweet and luscious. Usually these are served plain, and they need no garnish.

A sprinkling of lemon juice may be added, or brandy or an oloroso sherry. But why, when they are so delicious just as they are?

* * *

Other *fruta del tiempo* may include raspberries, apples, watermelon. *Ensalada de fruta*, a mixture of fresh fruits in season, or "fruit cup," as we call it, also may be offered for a *postre*.

Flan

FLAN AL CARAMELO (Caramel Custard)

8 tablespoons sugar	2 cups milk
1 teaspoon water	4 egg yolks or 3 whole eggs
	½ teaspoon vanilla

Place 6 tablespoons of the sugar and the water in a square Pyrex baking dish (10 by 10 inches), heat over very low heat, shaking occasionally to prevent burning, until sugar turns into golden syrup (or this can be done in a skillet and the syrup poured into 4 or 5 custard cups). Cool until firm. Combine milk, beaten egg yolk (or whole eggs, beaten), vanilla and remaining 2 tablespoons sugar, beat to blend well, pour over caramel. Place in larger pan with water to depth of ½ inch, bake at 325° for 1 to 1½ hours until knife inserted in center comes out clean. Chill again. Invert, turning out on platter. Cut large custard into squares to serve. Makes 4 to 6 servings.

FLAN AL RON (Rum Custard)

4 tablespoons sugar	Grated rind ½ orange
4 egg yolks	1¾ cups milk
2 teaspoons dark sweet rum	1 tablespoon honey

Caramelize sugar over low heat in baking dish as in recipe above, or place 1 tablespoon of the caramelized syrup in each of 4 custard cups; cool. Combine remaining ingredients, beat until smooth, pour over caramel. Bake in pan of hot water until firm, with oven set at 325°, for 1 to 1½ hours or until knife inserted in center comes out clean. Makes 4 servings.

FLAN CON CEREZA (Custard with Cherry Preserves)

Place 1 teaspoon cherry preserves in bottom of each custard cup. Make custard as for *Flan al Caramelo* (omitting caramelized sugar), pour over preserves and bake in same way.

FLAN DE COCO (Coconut Custard)

4 tablespoons sugar, caramelized

4 egg yolks

2 tablespoons sugar

½ cup orange juice

1½ cups milk

1 tablespoon cream sherry

Caramelize the sugar as in *Flan al Caramelo*; cool. Combine egg yolks, additional sugar, orange juice, milk, and sherry. Beat until smooth. Pour over cold caramel, bake in pan of hot water at 325° until firm or knife inserted in center comes out clean), about 1½ hours. Makes 4 servings.

Bizcocho y Tarta

BIZCOCHO (Basic Spongecake)

5 eggs, separated

1 cup sugar

1 cup sifted flour

½ teaspoon baking powder

Grated rind ½ lemon

Beat egg yolks until thick, slowly beat in sugar until fluffy. Sift combined flour and baking powder over yolks, beat just to blend thoroughly, stir in lemon rind. Beat egg whites until stiff; gently fold yolk mixture into whites. Pour into tube pan which has been *lightly* greased. Bake in preheated 350° oven for 30 to 35 minutes until cake springs back when pressed. Cool in pan 10 minutes, then turn out on cake rack. Serve plain, dusted with a mixture of cinnamon and confectioners' sugar, sprinkled with cream sherry, or in one of the following ways.

BIZCOCHO DE COCO (Coconut Spongecake)

1 recipe for bizcocho (above) *½ cup heavy cream (optional)*
½ cup shredded coconut *½ cup toasted blanched almonds, chopped*
Lemon filling (see below)

Make spongecake batter as in basic recipe, adding shredded coconut to yolk mixture. Divide batter into 2 layer pans which have been lined with waxed paper; bake in preheated 350° oven for 20 minutes, or until cake springs back when pressed. Cool in pan 10 minutes, turn out on racks. Spread lemon filling between layers and over top. Sprinkle almonds over top. If desired, whipped cream may be swirled around sides.

LEMON FILLING

½ cup sugar *½ teaspoon grated lemon rind*
2 tablespoons flour *2½ tablespoons lemon juice*
3 egg yolks *6 tablespoons orange juice*
⅓ cup water

Combine sugar and flour, add egg yolks, beat slightly, then add grated rind, juices, and water, beat just to blend well. Cook over hot water in top of double boiler until smooth and thickened. Cool before spreading on cake.

TARTA DE MOCHA

1 recipe for bizcocho *Grated German's sweet chocolate*
Mocha filling (see below) *½ cup heavy cream (optional)*

Make spongecake batter as for bizcocho (above), pour into 2 or 3 layer pans, bake in preheated 350° oven for 20 minutes or until cake springs back when pressed; let cool in pan 10 minutes after removing from oven, turn out on racks. Place mocha filling between layers; if three layers are made, spread whipped cream over top. Grate chocolate with coarse grater into curls, sprinkle these over top. (If the cake is baked in 2 layers, use mocha filling between layers and on top, whipped cream around sides.)

MOCHA FILLING

1⅔ cups sifted confectioners' sugar
½ cup butter
1 small square German's chocolate melted in:
3 tablespoons hot strong coffee
1 teaspoon gold or dark rum

Sift sugar; beat butter until creamy, gradually add sugar until smooth, then the chocolate and coffee. When slightly cooled, stir in rum.

BRAZO DE GITANO (Gypsy's Arm)

6 egg whites
4 egg yolks
¾ cup sugar
Grated rind 1 lemon
½ cup sifted flour

Line pan 13 by 9 inches with waxed paper, lightly grease the paper. Preheat oven to 375°. Beat egg whites until stiff. Separately beat egg yolks until thick; gradually beat in sugar, then lemon rind, and finally the flour until very smooth. Add whites to batter a third at a time, blending thoroughly to remove air bubbles. Pour batter into pan, spreading out evenly. Bake 15 minutes, or until cake springs back when touched. Loosen around edges with spatula, invert cake while hot on waxed paper sprinkled with confectioners' sugar. Spread filling over hot cake, roll up quickly, dust top with the sugar.

FILLING

¼ *cup sugar*
⅛ *teaspoon cinnamon*
1 *teaspoon cornstarch*

¼ *cup orange juice*
¼ *cup oloroso sherry*
1 *teaspoon brandy*
1 *egg yolk*

Blend sugar, cinnamon, and cornstarch, slowly beat in orange juice, sherry, and brandy, then egg yolk. Cook, stirring constantly, until thickened and smooth.

TOPPING

1 *cup heavy cream, whipped*
1 *tablespoon apricot jam*
1 *tablespoon brandy*

Whip cream until stiff. Thin jam with brandy, fold into cream.

MERENGUE DE TARTA JULIANCHU

Prepare cake as for *brazo de Gitano* (given above). Spread with date custard filling (below), roll up, keep moist until ready to cover with *merengue*.

DATE CUSTARD FILLING

½ *cup sugar*
⅓ *cup flour*

2 *cups milk, heated*
3 *egg yolks, beaten*
1 *cup pitted chopped dates*

Combine sugar and flour, stir in hot milk slowly, beating until smooth, add to eggs, beat again. Stir over hot water in double boiler until smooth and thickened. Cool in pan about 10 minutes. Add dates. Spread over sheet cake, roll up, keep cake moist in towel while preparing *merengue*.

MERENGUE

2½ cups sifted confectioners'   2 to 3 tablespoons cream
   sugar   2 egg whites, beaten stiff
2 teaspoons softened butter   ¼ cup crushed almonds

Beat butter until creamy, beat in sifted sugar a little at a
time, alternately with the cream, until smooth. (If necessary,
add a little water, no more than ½ teaspoon at a time, to give
frosting right consistency.) Separately beat egg whites until
stiff, fold frosting into egg whites, stirring gently until smooth.
Swirl over rolled-up cake. Sprinkle top with finely crushed
toasted almonds if desired.

* * *

The town of Ávila, a two-hour drive from Madrid, is a fascinating place to visit. Its medieval walls are still standing, all
its ninety-four towers looking just as they did in the sixteenth
century when St. Teresa lived here, walking out from Ávila
over rough country roads, tirelessly bent on reforming the nun-
neries, which, in that period of feudal wildness, had become
little more than homes for wayward girls or boardinghouses
for spinsters whose families had failed to acquire husbands
for them. St. Teresa built up the Carmelite order into a
force for reform; she was a defiant character with an earthy
sense of humor. She had mystic visions which she recorded
tirelessly on paper, writing all night long until her candle
gutted in its holder. It is also said she was prone to levitation
but fought against it because she preferred to remain earth-
bound. "Find God among the pots and pans," she urged her
followers, and it may have been during such a search that
these delicious little sweets which bear her name were created.

Avila was also the birthplace of another of Spain's famous
women: Isabella of Castile, who as queen led the country to
a period of great power and glory.

We sat on Ávila's main square, the Plaza Mayor, beyond its medieval portals, chewing on *yemas* with tea on a sunny February day, as peasants from the surrounding countryside tried to sell livestock and vegetables to townspeople. The yemas tasted so heavenly I determined to try them at home, but this type of confection is not easy for me to make. I had to make three tries before I succeeded. In flavor they were delicious, but frankly I would recommend them only to those who are skilled at candymaking.

Another version of yemas, quite foolproof, is made with mashed potatoes. These are not quite so good, but children seem to love them. They are called, appropriately, *yemas económicas.*

YEMAS DE SANTA TERESA

½ cup sugar
¼ cup water

Grated rind ½ lemon
Few drops lemon juice
5 large egg yolks

Boil sugar and water together until it begins to thicken; beat egg yolks with lemon juice and grated rind, add in a slow stream to the syrup, beating constantly; continue cooking over moderate heat 3 or 4 minutes, beating all the time. Remove from heat, continue to beat until it stiffens, then place the saucepan in a bowl of ice, beat until mixture is quite stiff. Pour at once into a pan lined with waxed paper, then, with rubber spatula, roll up edges to form one long thin roll. Chill in refrigerator until firm, almost hard. Cut with sharp knife into 1-inch pieces, roll these in palm of greased hand into small balls. Roll the balls in a mixture of confectioners' sugar and a pinch of cinnamon. Allow to dry out at room temperature.

YEMAS ECONOMICAS

1 *pound white potatoes,*	2 *cups sugar*
peeled and cooked	1 *pound almonds, blanched*
3 *whole eggs, beaten*	*and ground fine*

Mash potatoes or force through ricer. Beat eggs with sugar until thick, then add the mashed potatoes and the almonds ground fine in an electric blender or food grinder. Form into small round balls with palms of hand. Roll in confectioners' sugar, place on baking sheet covered with waxed paper; cover the yemas with more paper, dry thoroughly for 24 to 36 hours.

* * *

So many egg yolks are used in Spanish recipes I began to search around for something to do with egg whites, being a saving sort of person. The following *tarta de almendras* requires 14 whites, but then 7 egg yolks are needed as well. I guess the solution is to make individual meringues with the egg whites, to be served filled with canned peaches or ice cream. Peaches in meringue shells are delightful if sprinkled with oloroso sherry, then topped with a bit of whipped cream.

The grated almonds used in the following *tarta de almendras* taste surprisingly like coconut—I thought when I tasted this cake that there must be coconut in it. They are grated raw, *not* toasted.

TARTA DE ALMENDRAS (Almond Cake)

7 *egg yolks*	14 *egg whites*
1¼ *cups sugar*	1 *cup heavy cream*
4 *cups almonds, blanched,*	*Toasted almonds or grated*
grated or ground	*chocolate for garnish*

Beat egg yolks and sugar until very thick; add grated almonds. Beat egg whites until stiff, fold into yolk-nut mixture, pour into buttered and floured spring-form pan. Bake in preheated 350° oven for 40 to 45 minutes until cake tester (straw or toothpick) comes out clean. Cool in pan 10 minutes, release from pan onto rack. Top with whipped cream sweetened to taste and garnish with nuts or chocolate. Very rich.

GLORIAS (Sweet Potato Pastries)

These bear decided resemblance to our own sweet-potato pies. Since the Spanish recipe called for sweet potatoes to be cooked in a syrup, I decided that our canned Louisiana yams would do as well—and they did, made an easy short cut.

1 package pie-crust mix	½ cup blanched almonds,
1 teaspoon grated lemon peel	ground
1 can (1 pound) candied yams	¼ cup white or gold rum
	½ teaspoon cinnamon

Add lemon peel to pie crust mix (or make your own pastry according to your favorite recipe); roll out very thin. Cut into 3-inch circles. Meantime, heat the candied yams, add the ground almonds, rum, and cinnamon, blending well, beating to a purée (easy with electric blender or mixer). Place a spoonful of the sweet-potato mixture in each pastry circle, fold over, press edges together to seal, prick the top so steam may escape. Bake in preheated 400° oven until golden, about 25 minutes. Sprinkle while hot with confectioners' sugar.

* * *

While in Seville I so enjoyed a dessert called *crema de naranjas* I made a note of it as something Americans would like. It seemed to me to be a very delicious orange sherbet flavored with curaçao, frozen in an orange shell, which was quite pretty. Later, scanning Spanish cookbooks, I found several quite different recipes for *crema de naranjas*, so here are three for a choice.

CREMA DE NARANJAS (1) (Orange Cream)

6 large oranges	*1 tablespoon cornstarch*
1 cup orange juice	*2 egg yolks*
4 tablespoons sugar	*1 cup cream*

Slice top off oranges, cutting around the top in a saw-tooth pattern, if you like. Scoop out the pulp carefully, removing as much of the white membrane as you can while preserving the shape of the shells. Squeeze the fruit through a food mill or ricer to obtain juice, adding additional juice to make 1 cup. Strain carefully. Combine sugar, cornstarch, and egg yolks, beat until smooth, stir in orange juice and cream, cook and stir with whisk over hot water until thickened and smooth. Chill about 10 minutes, then pour into orange shells. Top each with a glacé cherry. Place in freezer or freezing compartment until firm. Serve to 6.

CREMA DE NARANJAS (2) (Orange Cream)

Scoop out 4 orange shells, as above, but fill with commercial orange sherbet (1 pint) which has been melted enough to add 1 or 2 tablespoons curaçao, then frozen once more to a mush. Place in freezer or freezing compartment until very firm, serve in the shells, garnished with glacé cherries.

CREMA DE NARANJAS (3) (Orange Cream)

1 envelope unflavored gelatin	*1¼ cups orange juice*
2 tablespoons sugar	*1 teaspoon curaçao*
2 egg yolks	*2 egg whites*
	1 cup heavy cream

In top of double boiler, combine gelatin, sugar, salt, and egg yolks, then slowly add orange juice. Cook over hot water, stirring, until mixture coats the spoon and is slightly thickened. Remove, chill until thickened to consistency of heavy cream. Beat egg whites until stiff; add curacao to custard, then fold in egg whites. Beat cream until stiff, fold in. Pour into 1½-quart mold or 6 to 8 individual molds. Chill until set, about 4 hours. Garnish with orange slices and glacé cherries.

MANZANAS FRITAS (Spanish Fried Apples)

These can be prepared at the table in an electric skillet and served piping hot.

3 apples, peeled and cored
3 tablespoons oloroso or cream
   sherry

3 tablespoons sugar
3 tablespoons flour
½ teaspoon cinnamon
¼ cup butter (4 tablespoons)

Cut apples in slices ¼ inch thick. Soak each slice in sherry, then roll in the mixture of sugar, flour, and cinnamon. Fry in butter until apples are tender and crisply golden on each side. Electric skillet should be set at 350°. Serve hot. Makes 4 to 6 servings.

TORRIJAS

This is a dessert always served at the beginning of Lent.

6 slices white bread, crusts
   trimmed
1 cup milk
2 tablespoons sugar

¼ cup olive oil or butter
2 tablespoons confectioners'
   sugar
½ teaspoon cinnamon

The bread is soaked in the milk and sugar until soft (as we prepare French toast, but usually no eggs are added). Then it is sautéed in oil until golden on each side. Immediately after removing from the pan, it is sprinkled with the confectioners' sugar and cinnamon blended together. While the Spanish always sauté the torrijas in oil, I personally prefer butter for this dish.

COMPOTA

½ pound dried prunes or figs   1 teaspoon grated orange rind
½ cup amontillado or oloroso   1 large can (1 pound 14
  sherry   ounces) whole apricots
1 cup apricot syrup (from   2 oranges, peeled and cut in
  canned apricots)   sections
¼ teaspoon cinnamon

Simmer prunes or figs in the sherry and apricot syrup; add cinnamon and grated orange rind. Simmer 15 minutes. Add the drained apricots and orange sections. Chill. Serve in sherbet glasses. Makes 8 servings.

FRUTA EN GELATINA AL JEREZ (Fruit Mold with Sherry)

2 envelopes unflavored gelatin   2 tablespoons lemon juice
¼ cup cold water   1¼ cups syrup from canned
1 cup boiling water   fruit
¼ cup sugar   3 cups fruit (peaches, pears,
1¼ cups oloroso sherry   grapes)

Soften gelatin in cold water, dissolve in boiling water; stir in sugar to dissolve. Add the sherry, lemon juice, and syrup from canned fruit. Pour gelatin mixture in 1½-quart mold, or in six 1-cup molds, or eight ¾-cup molds. Chill until consistency of egg white, add cut-up fruit, stir to distribute evenly, return to refrigerator. Or firm gelatin in layers, arranging fruit in pattern. When gelatin is firm throughout, unmold by dipping quickly in hot water, then turn out on platter. Serve with whipped cream flavored with sherry.

MARQUESA DE CHOCOLATE (Rich Chocolate Mousse)

¼ cup sugar   1 teaspoon vanilla
1 tablespoon flour   Grated peel ½ orange
4 eggs, separated   1½ cups heavy cream,
½ cup milk   whipped
12 tablespoons butter   ½ cup hazel nuts
6-ounce package semisweet
  chocolate

Lightly grease 1-quart mold. Combine sugar, flour, and egg yolks, stir in milk, heat, stirring with wire whisk over low heat until mixture is consistency of thin mayonnaise. Add butter a little at a time, stirring each addition until smooth. Remove from heat, add chocolate, vanilla, and orange peel. Stir until chocolate is melted. Cool. Pour into greased mold. Chill in refrigerator at least 5 hours. Unmold. Serve garnished with whipped cream sweetened to taste and hazel nuts. Makes 10 small but rich servings.

ARROZ CON LECHE (Rice Pudding)

This is a favorite dessert in north Spain, where there are many herds of cattle and milk is in plentiful supply. It seems characteristic of this part of Spain. I liked the following version because it is flavored with sherry or brandy (or Madeira), though as a dessert intended for children the liquor may be omitted and a teaspoon of vanilla used instead.

1 cup rice (short grain, preferably)
2 cups water
½ teaspoon salt
4 cups milk

Grated rind ½ lemon
1 tablespoon oloroso sherry or sweet Spanish brandy
4 tablespoons granulated sugar
2 tablespoons brown sugar

Cover rice with water and salt, bring to a boil, boil hard 5 minutes; drain. Add milk, lemon rind, and sherry or brandy, let milk come slowly just to the boil, lower heat, simmer gently 10 minutes. Add sugar, cook until liquid is absorbed, about 20 minutes longer. Cool, then spoon into serving dish, chill 2 hours or longer. Sprinkle with brown sugar, put under broiler until sugar has caramelized; serve at once. (¼ teaspoon cinnamon is sometimes mixed with the brown sugar.) Serve with cream. Makes 6 to 8 servings.

AMOR FRIO (Cold Love)

Here is our old friend Spanish cream, a recipe which appeared in every American cookbook in the early part of our century.

1 envelope unflavored gelatin	1 cup mixed fruit
¼ cup sugar	¼ cup gold rum or oloroso
¼ teaspoon salt	sherry
⅛ teaspoon cinnamon	2 tablespoons confectioners'
4 egg yolks	sugar
2¼ cups milk	4 egg whites, beaten stiff
	½ cup heavy cream

Mix gelatin, sugar, salt, and cinnamon, place in top of double boiler with egg yolks; slowly add milk. Stir over hot water until mixture coats spoon. Meantime, marinate fruit in rum or sherry and in confectioners' sugar. Refrigerate custard mixture until it thickens slightly, stir in fruit (do not drain). Replace in refrigerator while beating egg whites until stiff. Separately beat cream until stiff. Fold cream into custard mixture first, then carefully fold in egg whites. Pour into 1½-quart mold, chill until firm. Makes 12 servings.

MERMELADA DE TOMATES (Tomato Marmalade)

This is a simply wonderful sweet, good on toast, even can be spooned over ice cream!

2 cups tomatoes, skinned, quartered	2 cups sugar
1 seeded lemon, put through grinder	¼ cup oloroso sherry

Combine all ingredients, let stand 2 hours. Bring to a boil, stir frequently until syrup is thick (falls in large slow drops from end of spoon). Remove from heat, add another 2 tablespoons sherry, pour into 5 sterilized jelly glasses.

Index

Index

Albóndigas, 35
 de Lomo, 137
Alcachofas: con Arroz, 110
 Ensalada de, 40
 à la Granadina, 161
 con Jamón, 40
 Salteadas, 161
Ali-Oli Sauce, 96
Almejas: con Arroz, 111
 à la Marinera, 30
Almond: Cake, 194
 Salad Dressing, 175
Almonds, Toasted, 31
Amor Frío, 200
Andaluz, 28
Aperitivos, 21–42
Appetizers: 29–42
 Álbóndigas, 35
 Alcachofas, 160–62
 Almejas à la Marinera, 30
 Almonds, Toasted, 31
 Artichokes, 35, 160–62
 with Ham, 40
 Artichoke Salad, 41
 Buñuelitos de Jamón, 36
 Cheese Delights, 33
 Chicken Livers Brochette, 32
 Chicken Salad, 35
 Clam Salad, 34
 Clams à la Marinera, 30
 Cocktail Meat Balls, 35
 Dates with Bacon, 36
 Delicias de Queso, 33
 Empanaditas de Ternera, 35
 Emparedados de Jamón y Queso, 33
 Ensalada: de Alcachofas, 41
 de Atún, 30
 de Langosta, 38
 Ensaladilla: de Almejas, 34
 de Pollo, 35
 Russa, 34
 Fiambres, 42
 Fish Pâté, 40
 Fried Peppers, 42

Gambas: al Ajillo, 29
 Empanadas, 36
 al Jerez, 31
Ham and Cheese Canapés, 33
Ham Fritters, 36
Hígados de Pollo, 32
Huevos Rellenos, 32
Langostinas Vinagreta, 31
Lemon-Stuffed Olives, 34
Lenguados Fritos, 33
Lobster Salad, 38
Meat Pâté, 39
Medianoches, 32
Onion Tart, 37
Pescado Escabeche, 41
Pimientos Fritos, 42
Prensado: de Carne, 39
 de Pescado, 40
Russian Salad Canapés, 34
Salmón Ahumado, 34
Sardinas en Cazuela, 32
Shrimp: Batter-Fried, 36
 with Garlic, 29
 in Sherry Sauce, 31
 Vinaigrette, 31
Stuffed Eggs, 32
Stuffed Tomatoes, 38
Smoked Salmon, 34
Tarta de Cebolla, 37
Tomates: Ali-oli, 39
 Rellenos, 38
Tuna Salad, 30
Veal Pastries, 35
Apples, Spanish Fried, 197
Arroz: à la Valenciana, 102–5
 Alicantina, 110
 con Habas, 113
 con Leche, 199
 à la Marinera, 111
 con Mariscos y Lomo, 108
 con Pollo, 109
 Primavera, 112
 See also Paella
Artichokes: Cooking of, 160
 Granada Style, 161

with Ham, 40, 161
with Rice, 110
Salad, 41
Asparagus Omelet, 70
Aves, 141–57

Bacalao: à la Vizcaína, 93
de Alcántara, 94
Baked Ham with Candied Egg Yolk,
135
Baked Stuffed Tomatoes, 72
Bananas in Rum Sauce, 186
Basque Linoyada, 29
Bass: Baked in Foil, 89
à la Pastelera, 90
Beans: Green, Spanish Style, 166
Mountain Style, 167
Béchamel Sauce, 101
Beef: Bullfighter's Steak, 130
Fillet of, Gredos, 129
Intoxicated, 132
Pot Roast, 131
Pot Roast Castilian Style, 132
Berenjenas: Caserta, 164
à la Española, 163
Preparation of, 162
Rellenas à la Andaluz, 164
Señorito, 163
Birds, 141–57
Bisque, Shellfish, 54
Bizcocho y Tarta, 188–89
de Coco, 189
Brains, Calf's, 140
Brandied Oranges, 181
Brazo de Gitano, 190–1
Bullfighter's Steak, 130
Bullfighter's Stuffed Fish, 88
Buñuelitos de Jamón, 36

Cadera de Vaca à la Castellana, 132
Cadera de Toro, 130
Cake. See Bizcocho; Tarta
Calabacines Rellenos, 165
Calabaza à la Española, 165
Caldereta de Cordero al Jerez, 118
Caldo Gallego, 57
Calf's Brains, 140
Candied Egg Yolk, 136
Caramel Custard, 187
Carne Borracha, 132
Carnes, 114–40
Castilian Pot Roast, 132
Catalan Vegetable Soup, 55

Catalonian Seafood Casserole, 81
Cauliflower: Fried, 170
Vinaigrette, 170
Cazuela de Habas à la Granadina, 64
Cegalas en Gelatina, 79
Cheese Delights, 33
Charcoal-grilled Steaks, 122
Cherry Custard, 188
Chicken: Aragon Style, 144
Bilbao Style, 150
Breasts, Catalan Style, 148
Breasts with Almonds, 145
Breasts in the Style of Philip II,
155
Casserole, Sherry Sauce, 151
Chilindrón, 149
Fricassee: Seville Style, 147
Fricassee, Spicy, 142
Fried, Marinated in Sherry Sauce,
145
Fried, à la Tenerife, 147
Livers Brochette, 32
with Oranges, 146
Pepitoria, 142
with Rice, 109
Salad, 35
in Sherry Sauce, 145
Spicy, Fricassee, 142
Stuffed, 143
Tropical Style, 151
with Vegetables, 146
Chick-Peas: with Ham, 169
Seville Style, 168
Soup, 56
Stew, 138
Chocolate Mousse, 198–99
Chuletas: de Cerdo a la Aragonesa,
133
à la Julianchu, 122–23
con Salsa de Tomates, 134
de Ternera Capricho, 126
Clam Salad, 34
Clams: à la Marinera, 30
with Rice, 111
Clear Consommé, 48
Cochifrito, 119
Cocido, 138
Coconut: Custard, 188
Spongecake, 188
Cold Garlic Soup, 51
Codfish: Alcántara Style, 94
Salt, Vizcaya Style, 93

Coliflor: Frito, 170
à la Vinagreta, 170
Cold Love, 200
Compota: de Melocotón, 182
Mixed, 198
Coñac, 27
Consomé: Madrileño, 49
Sencillo, 48
Consommé, Clear, 48
Corderito Asado à la Castellana, 117
Cordero: Asado à la Casa Botin, 117
à la Chilindrón, 120
Crab-Meat Omelet, 69
Crema de Mariscos, 54
Crema de Naranjas (1), (2), (3),
196
Cuban-Style Eggs, 62
Custard: 187–88
Caramel, 187
with Cherry Preserves, 188
Coconut, 188
Rum, 187

Dates with Bacon, 36
Dátiles con Bacón, 36
Delicias de Queso, 33
Desserts: Amor Frío, 200
Arroz con Leche, 199
Bananas in Rum Sauce, 186
Brazo de Gitano, 190
Bizcocho, 188
Bizcocho de Coco, 189
Caramel Custard, 187
Cherry Custard, 187
Coconut Custard, 188
Compota, 198
Compota de Melocotones, 182
Crema de Naranjas, 196
Figs, 184
Flan, 187–88
Fresas, 185
Fruta en Gelatina, 198
Glorias, 195
Gypsy's Arm, 190
Melon, 186
Pineapple with Kirsch, 185
Plátanos al Ron, 186
Merengue de Tarta Julianchu, 191
Peaches, 182–83
Naranjas, 181
Tarta de Almendras, 194
Tarta de Mocha, 189
Yemas, 193–94

Drinks, 26–29
Duck: with Olives, 153
with Oranges, 152

Eggplant:
Baked, Young Master, 163
Casserole, 164
Preparation of, 162
Spanish Style, 163
Stuffed, 163
Eggs: Baked in Tomato Sauce, 64
Basque Style, 73
Béchamel, 61
Candied, 136
Cuban Style, 62
with Eggplant, 63
Flamenco, 63
Gypsy Style, 64
in Ramekins, 60
Piperade, 73
al Plato, 60
Puffed, 72
Rioja Style, 64
Scrambled, with Mushrooms, 62
Scrambled, with Tomato, 61
Seville Style, 71
Stuffed, 32
Empanaditas de Ternera, 35
Emparedados de Jamón y Queso, 33
Ensalada: de Alcachofas, 41
de Atún, 30
de Boquerón y Aceituna, 177
de Langosta, 38
de Legumbres, 173
Mixta, 176
de Tomates, 175
Tropical, 175
Valenciana, 176
Ensaladilla: de Almejas, 34
de Pollo, 35
Russa, 34
Entremesas, 29–42
Escalopes de Ternera, 127
Escalope Zíngara, 128
Espinacas: y Huevos à la Granadina,
68
Preparation of, 174
Estofado de Vaca, 131

Fabada Asturiana, 12
Figs: Fresh, in Málaga Wine, 184
in Syrup with Ice Cream, 184
Filete Gredos, 129

Filete de Lenguado Relleno, 86–87
Fillet of Beef Gredos, 192
Fillet of Sole Ybarra, 87
Fish: Baker Style, 90
  Bullfighter's Stuffed, 88
  Mountain Style, 89
  Pâté, 40
  Pickled, 41
  in Sherry Sauce, 83
  Soup, 53
  Steak in Sherry Sauce, 83
  Steaks Basque Style, 82
  Tropical, 86
  See also Pescado y Mariscos; Appetizers
Fish and Shellfish, 74–101
Flaming Partridges, 157
Flan: al Caramelo, 187
  col Cereza, 188
  de Coco, 188
  al Ron, 187
Fresas, 185
Fried: Fillet (fish), 90
  Pimientos, 42
  Sole, 33
Fruit, 180–87
Fruit Mold with Sherry, 198
Fruta en Gelatina al Jerez, 198

Gallina: à la Bilbaína, 150
  en Cazuela al Jerez, 151
  à la Sevillana, 147
Gambas: al Ajillo, 29
  Empanadas, 36
  al Jerez, 31
Garbanzos: con Jamón, 169
  Potaje de, 56
  à la Sevillana, 168
Garlic Sauce, 96
Garlic Soup: Cold, with Melon or
    Grapes, 51
  Hot, 50
Gazpacho, 43–47
  Andaluz, 47
  Sevillano, 46
  Valenciana, 46
Glorias, 195
Granadas, 185
Green Beans: Pickled, 174
  Spanish Style, 166
Guisado de Pescados, 53
Guisantes à la Vasca, 167

Gypsy Style Eggs, 64
Gypsy's Arm, 190–91

Habas a la Montanesa, 167
Ham: with Candied Egg Yolk, 135–36
  and Cheese Canapés, 33
  Fritters, 36
  Serrano, 14
Hash, 134
Hígado à la Asturiana, 139
Hígados de Pollo, 32
Higos: en Almíbar con Helado, 184
  con Vino Malagueño, 184
Hors d'Oeuvres. *See* Appetizers
Hot Garlic Soup, 50
Huevos: Arriba, 72
  con Berenjenas, 63
  à la Cubana, 62
  à la Flamenca, 63
  Hilado, 136
  al Plato, 60
  Revueltos con Champinones, 62
  Revueltos con Tomate, 61
  à la Riojana, 64
  à la Sevillana, 71
  à la Zíngara, 64

Intoxicated Beef, 131

Jamón Asado con Huevos Hilado,
    135–36
Jerez, 22–26, 28–29
Judías Verdes: Escabeche, 174
  à la Española, 166

Lamb: Chops with Ali-oli Sauce,
    119
  Chilindrón, 120
  Cochifrito, 119
  Fricassee of, with Artichokes, 119
  Kidneys, 135
  Kidneys Navarra Style, 139
  Larded, 118
  Roast, Casa Botín, 116
  Stew, Jerez Style, 118
  Stew, Levantine Style, 120
  Suckling, Roasted in Castilian
    Style, 117
Langosta Perpignan, 79–80
Langostinos: à la Marina, 77
  al Champán, 78
  al Jerez, 77

Legumbres y Ensaladas, 158–77
  Vinagreta, 31
Lemonade, Basque, 29
Lemon-Stuffed Olives, 34
Lenguado: Relleno, 86
  Ybarra, 87
Lenguados: al Champán, 78
  Filete de, Relleno, 86
  Fritos, 33
Lima-Bean Casserole Granada Style, 64
Liver Asturian Style, 139
Lobina en Papel, 89
Lobster: Perpignan Style, 79–80
  Salad, 38
Loin of Pork with Mushroom Stuffing, 133
Lomo Trufado con Champiñones, 133

Málaga Wine, 27
Manzanas Fritas, 197
Marquesa de Chocolate, 198–99
Mayonesa, 100
Mayonnaise, 100
Meat Balls, 35
  Pork, 137
Meat Pâté, 39
Mechada de Cordero, 118
Medianoches, 32
Melon, 186–87
Melocotones: en Almíbar, 182
  Compota de, 182
  con Helado, 182
  con Vino Blanco, 183
Menestra: de Cordero Levantina, 120
  de Legumbres, 173
Merengue de Tarta Julianchu, 191
Merluza: al Jerez, 83
  Koskera, 82
  Tronco de Tropical, 86
  Tropical, 86
Mermelada de Tomates, 200
Mero:
  à la Montaña, 89
  à la Pastelera, 90
Mint Dressing, 176
Mixed Seafood Salad, 176
Mocha Tart, 189
Mock Partridges, 124
Mousse, Chocolate, 198

Naranjas: al Coñac, 181
  al Vino Tinto, 181

Olive and Anchovy Salad, 177
Olive oil, Spanish, 18–19
Olives, Lemon-Stuffed, 34
Omelets: with Asparagus, 70
  with Beans, 70
  Crab-Meat, 69
  Potato, 69
  Sacromonte, 67
  Springtime, 71
  with Squash, 71
Onion Tart, 37
Oranges: Brandied, 181
  in Red Wine, 181

Paella: Without Bones, 107
  à la Catalonia, 106
  à la Valenciana, 102–6
Parellade, 107
Partridges: Flamed, 157
  Innkeeper Style, 156
  in the Style of Philip II, 155
Pastries. *See* Bizcocho; Tarta; Glorias
Patatas à la Castellana, 168
Pâté: Fish, 40
  Meat, 39
Pato: à la Sevillana, 153
Pato: con Naranjas, 152
  à la Sevillana, 153
Peaches: Compote, 182
  with Ice Cream, 182
  in Syrup, 182
  in White Wine, 183
Pears, 183
Peas Basque Style, 167
Pechugas de Pollo: à la Catalana, 148
  con Salsa de Almendras, 145
Peppers: Sautéed, 42
  Stuffed, 169
Pepitoria de Gallina, 142
Perdices del Capellán, 125
Perdiz: Felipe Segundo, 155
  à la Mesonera, 156
  Sobre Canapé, 157
Pescado: Escabeche, 41
  Frito, 90
  Relleno al Toreador, 88
Pescados y Mariscos, 74–101
Pez Espada, 91
Picadillo, 134
Pickled Fish, 41

Pickled Green Beans, 166
Pimientos: Fried *Fritos*, 42
  Rellenos, 169
  Stuffed, 169
Piña al Kirsch, 185
Piperade, 73
Pisto: (1), (2), 171
  Manchego, 172
Plátanos, 186
Pollo: *à la Aragonesa*, 144
  con Arroz, 109
  al Ast, 149–50
  Chilindrón, 149
  Frito al Jerez, 145
  Frito à la Tenerife, 147
  à la Jardinera, 146
  con Naranja, 146
  Pechugas de, con Salsa de Almendras, 145
  Relleno, 143
  à la Sevillana, 147
  Tropical, 151
Pomegranates, 185
Pork: Chops Aragonese Style, 133
  Chops in Tomato Sauce, 134
  Hash, 134
  Loin of, with Mushroom Stuffing, 133
  Meat Balls, 137
  Roast, Mushroom Stuffing, 133
Postres, 178–200
Potaje de Garbanzos, 56
Potatoes Castilian Style, 168
Potato Omelet, 69
Prensado: *de Carne*, 39
  de Pescado, 40
Puffed Eggs, 72
Pulpetas, 125

Quarter-of-an-Hour Soup, 52

Rapsodia de Mariscos, 80
Rape, 76
Rhapsody of Shellfish, 80
Rice: Alicante Style, 110
  Artichokes with, 110
  with Beans, 113
  with Chicken, 109
  Clams with, 111
  Fisherman's Style, 111
  Pudding, 199
  with Shellfish and Pork, 108
  Springtime, 112

Riñones: *de Cordero à la Señorita*, 135
  à la Navarra, 139
Roast Lamb Casa Botín, 116
Roast Pork, Mushroom Stuffing, 133
Romesco Sauce, 99
Royal Soup, 48
Rum Custard, 187
Russian Salad Canapé, 34

Salad: Chicken, 35
  Clam, 34
  Lobster, 38
  Mixed Seafood (1), (2), 176–77
  of Cooked Vegetables, 173
  of Tomatoes, 175
  Olive and Anchovy, 177
  Tropical Fruit, 175
  Valencia Style, 176
Salad Dressings: Almond, 175
  Mint, 176
  Spanish rule for, 159
Salmon: Baked in Sauce, 92
  Smoked, 34
Salmón: *Ahumado*, 34
  al Horno, 92
Salsas: *à la Granadina*, 99
  de Aceite, 97
  Ali-oli, 96
  de Almendras, 175
  Amarilla, 98
  Colorada, 99
  de Espinacas, 97
  Hernandez, 96
  de Menta, 176
  Romesco, 99
  de Tomate, 96
  Verde I, II, 98
Salt cod, *Vizcaya Style*, 93
Sandwich Snacks, 32–33
Sangría, 28–29
Sardinas en Cazuela, 32
Sardines in Casserole, 32
Sauces:
  Béchamel, 101
  Garlic, 96
  Granada, 99
  Green, I, II, 98
  Olive-Oil, 97
  Raw Spinach, 97
  Red, 99
  Romesco, 99

Tomato, 96
Yellow, 98
Scrambled Eggs: with Eggplant, 63
  with Mushrooms, 62
  with Tomatoes, 61
Seafood Casserole Catalonian, 81
Seafood Rhapsody, 80
Seafood Soup of Málaga, 51
Sesos Rebozados, 140
Shellfish. See also Clams;
  Shrimp; Lobster
Shellfish Bisque, 54
Sherry, 22–26
Sherry Drinks, 26, 28–29
Shrimp: à la Marina, 77
  al Jerez, 77
  Batter-Fried, 36
  in Aspic, 79
  in Champagne Sauce, 78
  in Sherry Sauce, 31
  Large, in Sherry Sauce, 77
  Large, Seashore Style, 77
  Vinaigrette, 31
  with Garlic, 29
Sole: Fillets Ybarra, 87
  Fried, 33
  in Champagne Sauce, 78
  in Sherry Sauce, 83
  Stuffed Fillets of, 86
  Tropical, 86
Sopa: de Ajo, 50
  de Ajo Blanco, 51
  Castellana Siglo XIV, 58
  de Catalonia, 55
  de Cuarto de Hora, 52
  Malagueña, 51
  Real, 48
Soups: Castellana Siglo XIV, 58
  Catalan Vegetable, 55
  Chick-Pea, 56
  Cold Garlic, with Melon or
    Grapes, 51
  Fish, 53
  in 14th-Century-Castilian Style, 58
  Garlic, 50–1
  Gazpacho, 43–47
  Hot Garlic, 50
  of Galicia, 57
  Onion, Spanish, 49
  Quarter-of-an-Hour, 52
  Royal, 48
  Seafood, of Málaga, 51

Shellfish Bisque, 54
Spanish Onion, 49
  See also Consomé
Spanish Brandy (Coñac), 27
Spanish Cream, 200
Spanish Olive Oil, 18–9
Spanish Onion Soup, 49
Spanish Mayonnaise, 100
Spanish Screwdriver, 28
Spanish Sherry. See Sherry
Spicy Chicken Fricassee, 142
Spinach: and Eggs Granada Style, 68
  preparation of, 174
Spongecake: Basic, 188
  Coconut, 189
Spring Omelet, 71
Springtime Rice, 112
Squash: Omelet, 71
  Spanish Style, 165
  Stuffed, Baby, 165
Strawberries, 185
Stuffed: Eggs, 32
  Eggplant, 163–64
  Filet of Sole, 86
  Peppers, 169
  Swordfish, 91
  Tomatoes, 38
  Tomatoes, Baked, 72
Suckling Lamb Roasted in Castilian
  Style, 117
Sweet Potato Pastries, 195

Tapas. See Appetizers
Tarta: de Almendras, 194
  de Cebolla, 37
  de Helado, 179
  de Merengue Julianchu, 191
  de Mocha, 189
Ternera: Cazuela, 123
  con Naranja, 127
  Salteada al Jerez, 124
Toasted Almonds, 31
Tomates: Ali-oli, 39
  Rellenos, 38
  Rellenos al Horno, 72
Tomato: Marmalade, 200
  Salad, 175
Tomatoes: Baked Stuffed, 72
  Stuffed, 38
Torrijas, 197
Tortilla: con Calabacines, 71
  de Cangrejo, 69
  con Espárragos, 70

con *Halsas*, 70
con *Patatas*, 69
Primovera, 71
al *Sacromonte*, 67
Tronco de Merluza Tropical, 86
Tropical Fruit Salad, 175
Trout in the Style of Philip V, 91
Truchas Felipe V, 91
Tuna Salad, 30

Veal: Birds, 125
Chops Caprice, 126
Hash (Picadillo), 134
in Casserole, 123

in Orange Sauce, 127
Mock Partridges, 125
Pastries, 35
Scallopini Gypsy Style, 128
Scallopini in Sherry Sauce, 124
Scallopini with Zucchini, 127
Steaks, Charcoal-Grilled, 122
Vegetables: 158–77
Stew of Andalusia, 173

Yemas: de Santa Teresa, 193
Económicas, 194

Zarzuela de Mariscos, 81